CALIFORNIA Madams

By Sherry Monahan

FARCOUNTRY
PRESS

Dedication

For Larry. But also to my female ancestors who may have chosen this profession—whether as a need to survive or by their own choosing. Regardless, I'm here because of them.

Acknowledgments

I would like to extend a heartfelt thanks to Renato Rodriguez at the San Diego History Center, to Wendy Figueroa at San Diego's Mount Hope Cemetery, to Delphine Petit Vayron for her French translations, and to the research librarians at the North Baker Research Library, San Francisco. And to my husband, who patiently listens and assists.

ISBN: 978-1-56037-659-0

Cover photograph courtesy of Legends of America.
Back cover photograph of Maurisia Duarte courtesy of Leonard Turnbull.

For more information about our books, write Farcountry Press, P.O. Box 5630, Helena, MT 59604; call (800) 821-3874; or visit www.farcountrypress.com.

Library of Congress Cataloging-In-Publication data on file.

Produced and printed in the United States of America.

23 22 21 20 19   1 2 3 4 5

Table of Contents

Introduction

Warning! Some of the stories in this book, while true, may disgust you and possibly give you nightmares—they did me. To avoid this, stay away from Lizzie the Flea and Lee Francis.

Addressing someone as "madam" in California during the 19th century was quite proper. However, calling someone a madam was a completely different matter. The first was respectable and the other was far from it. Another proper Victorian term was *parlor*, a room where sophisticated ladies in their laced-up corsets, gowns, and gloves sipped coffee and ate tea sandwiches. However, most of these proper women wouldn't have dared step into a *parlor house*, which was just another name for a brothel or bordello.

Men of all social levels, and even some women, went to parlor houses for things they couldn't get at home. More often than not, it was just plain sex—nothing too kinky. These men were either bachelors living in remote areas or married men who wanted to cheat on their wives for various reasons. That's not to say that some clients didn't want to get their freak on, but that wasn't the most common request. As towns grew and evolved, so did their brothels. Many offered all types of prostitutes, including men as well as women, all races, and even girls and boys of all ages. Some houses offered threeways, bestiality, sodomy, and homosexual and lesbian sex in addition to their regular services, but they were fewer in number. Oftentimes, the madam needed to hire girls who were willing to be "creative," as one madam called it, for special requests.

The brothels themselves came in various shapes and sizes, and establishments ranged from lowly cribs to high-end mansions or parlor houses. The higher-end brothels had their own hierarchy and were often referred to as either "low" or "high" houses. Because of the social implications, red-light or tenderloin districts were segregated from the respectable parts of town. They were often found in poorer areas or "on the other side of the tracks." But there was always at least one madam who was willing to tempt fate and open her business in the proper part of town. These women were often outed and maligned in the papers and on the streets until they were pressured into moving. And yes, they really did use red lights to notify customers what type of business they were. At night, the red light glowed and flickered, as if it was subliminally luring customers in. During the day, a red cloth was draped in front of a window, door, or transom and was sometimes illuminated with a lamp to enhance it. Regardless of location, many houses of ill fame were opened under the guise of a lodging house, and the madam was the proprietor.

California had all of these, but in its early years it was rough, rowdy, and full of men. It was men who came to the mining camps and other outposts, and these places—like most start-up western towns—had more than their share of lonely men looking for any distraction. Some places were known as "stag towns" because of the lack of women.

Prostitutes—women of the night, soiled doves, or sporting girls—followed the men and the money. Many arrived in California during the gold rush era to meet the lonely miners' demand for companionship. Once the population of towns began to expand, a greater number of people needed more services. Ladies of the evening began opening brothels all over California.

Some turned tricks on their own, and some were managed by pimps or *maquereaux*, the French word for pimps; it was often shortened to Macs. Most madams didn't want girls with Macs because they could be troublesome. In many cases, the girls managed by madams were considered high-end and imported from France and other European countries. Several madams offered black girls because they were considered forbidden fruit; Chinese girls were viewed as exotic pleasures.

These women had left their families, and they used aliases to avoid shame. Young prostitutes chose nicknames, and many a Mattie, Hattie, Lizzie, Kate, Maggie, and Lottie could be found in brothels. Older madams, on the other hand, saw this as a business and frequently used their actual names, although aliases sometimes came in handy. Some madams were kind, generous, and charitable, while others were downright nasty and ruthless characters.

Some women saw prostitution as a way to earn big money in a short period of time. Employment options for single or widowed women were extremely limited—understandably, there were those who didn't want to toil over dirty laundry or scrub floors for little pay. These were the women who chose to be in the business. But not all girls and women in brothels chose their way of life, and some were duped into it. Many madams either traveled to New York or hired a procurer (men and women alike played this role) there to wait for young, vulnerable women to arrive from foreign countries. After disembarking from their ships, the new arrivals made their way through customs. Madams or procurers with a keen sense spotted the wide-eyed girls who were full of dreams. These naïve girls were promised respectable jobs in homes as maids or other domestic positions in exchange for their passage to the West. After traveling cross country, they found themselves indebted and bound to a life of prostitution. Most did not understand the laws and did not know how to fight the fraud that entrapped them.

Sometimes these women, most often the youngest girls, were rescued when someone turned the madams into the authorities. The girls would tell of their harrowing journeys and forced life of prostitution. If they were underage, they were removed and taken to asylums or industrial schools for reform and protection. If they were adults, they were set out on their own. It was difficult for many of the young girls because most of them had no family and were faced with the harsh reality of living in a house for the insane, with shoddy clothes and horrid food.

Many madams cared for their girls and fed them well, dressed them in the finest clothes, and ensured they had regular medical check-ups. When given the choice between the two, the young girls often chose to go back to their madam and live out their servitude in luxury. In the case of a seventeen-year-old San Francisco girl named Olivia Loebel, she chose a marriage proposal as a third option. She was engaged to Henry Griffin, and when she was arrested at Alice Stewart's brothel on Quincy Place in 1889, Griffin awaited his betrothed's release from prison. Olivia was supposed to testify against Stewart, but the judge deliberated on whether or not to grant Olivia bail. Given the complication of her being a minor, the judge pondered the options of letting her marry someone who seemed to be in love with her or sending her to an industrial school. She told the judge she would marry just about anyone to get out of prison.[1]

The fate of many of these women is impossible to trace, as if they never existed, because so many used aliases. More often than not, these women were remembered by history because prostitutes and madams made the newspapers for a variety of reasons. Once they left the business, they vanished from the historical record due to death, marriage, or a change of names.

There are enough madams in California's history for two books, if not more. I've chosen to delve deeper into the lives of the women whose stories haven't been written about as extensively as others. I would be remiss, however, if I didn't include—at least briefly—some of the most colorful characters in California's madam history.

1

Greater San Francisco

San Francisco was a city teeming with pioneers from all walks of life, and the Barbary Coast had sophisticated men in top hats, pick-wielding miners, salty seamen, and the women who served them all with untold pleasures. The Barbary Coast and Tenderloin districts soon emerged, where sex and debauchery could be found on every corner and in dark alleys. The Tenderloin contained the streets of O'Farrell, Eddy, Turk, Powell, Larkin, Morton (now Maiden), Ellis, and others that ran between Geary and Market. The Barbary Coast was in the northeastern part of the city, encompassing both sides of Broadway and Pacific Avenue and the cross streets between them, from Stockton Street to the waterfront. Author Benjamin Estelle Lloyd spared no vice when he described the Barbary Coast in 1876:[2]

> The Barbary Coast is the haunt of the low and the vile of every kind. The petty thief, the house burglar, the tramp, the whore monger, lewd women, cut-throats, murderers, are all found

Women of the Barbary Coast, 1890. PHOTOGRAPH COURTESY OF THE SAN FRANCISCO HISTORY CENTER, SAN FRANCISCO PUBLIC LIBRARY.

here. Dance halls and concert-saloons, where blear-eyed men and faded women drink vile liquor, smoke offensive tobacco, engage in vulgar conduct, sing obscene songs and say and do everything to heap upon themselves more degradation, are numerous. Low gambling houses, thronged with riot-loving rowdies, in all stages of intoxication, are there. Opium dens, where heathen Chinese and God-forsaken men and women are sprawled in miscellaneous confusion, disgustingly drowsy or completely overcome, are there. Licentiousness, debauchery, pollution, loathsome disease, insanity from dissipation, misery, poverty, wealth, profanity, blasphemy, and death, are there. And Hell, yawning to receive the putrid mass, is there also.

Many people knew of the wanton ways of the women who peddled flesh in their city, but so long as it didn't invade their Victorian piety, most looked the other way. While lawmakers and citizens couldn't control all the houses of assignation in town, they could try to set some limits. In 1872, Benjamin Tuttle, a state assemblyman from Sonoma County, introduced legislation to make it a crime for anyone to procure, entice, or invite any unmarried female under the age of twenty-five into a house of ill fame to have illicit carnal connection with any man. The penalty for violating this was punishable by imprisonment for one year or a $1,000 fine. He wrote, "There is no punishment too severe for the man who leads an innocent young girl from the paths of virtue, and if this bill, the full text of which has not reached us, provides a means of prevention for such crimes, it will be hailed with joy by all who have the good rising generation at heart."[3]

The following year, in 1873, the new chief of police, Theodore G. Cockrill, issued an order about houses of ill fame. He advised his officers who covered the disreputable beats to ensure that the houses did not violate the public decency law. Specifically, the order was aimed at preventing the working girls from standing in doorways and windows, or on the streets, to entice customers. Chief Cockrill held his officers responsible for enforcing the laws.[4] Apparently that didn't last too long—by 1887, citizens were outraged by the brothels on Morton between Kearny and Stockton, on Berry off Grant, and on Dupont between Bush and Pine. The brazen women who worked in these establishments were accused of hanging out their windows half-naked with painted faces. Their reckless behavior of sitting at pianos playing and singing lewd songs enraged some, as did those who stood in the doorways with tights showing their voluptuous figures. They teased and fraternized with young messenger boys and police alike. A writer to the *San Francisco Vindicator* stated that one brothel in particular stood out as obnoxious. The Rose Bud at 308 Grant Avenue was called one of the most disreputable "dives" in the city. Instead of stopping the music at 1 A.M., which was required by the ordinance, they played until two, three, and sometimes four in the morning "while prostitutes of the most disreputable order [were] dancing inside and standing at the door."[5]

It wasn't until the 1890s that the demimonde fully felt the pressure of legislation and laws, forcing the women to find creative ways to

Carousing in the Barbary Coast. PHOTOGRAPH COURTESY OF THE SAN FRANCISCO HISTORY CENTER, SAN FRANCISCO PUBLIC LIBRARY.

entice clients to their locations. Some were prostitutes on their own, while other had pimps or madams to manage them. The *San Francisco Chronicle* called attention to its opposing paper's classified ad section where prostitution was offered in plain sight. The *Chronicle* opined the *Examiner's* ads were barely subtle, and most knew what they were for when women advertised their massage services at various hotels and apartments in the city. The early ads were detailed, offering "vapor baths," "Arabian baths," "magnetic treatments," and more.

In addition to advertising their services, many madams let it be known they were hiring young assistants or ladies to work in massage parlors. They were particularly fond of stating where they hailed from, as in: "Arrived—Mrs. Williams, from Australia; massage." They would include their street address and room number. After the ads appeared for several months and everyone knew what they were for, the women simply listed their name, address, and "massage." Some

The Nucleus Hotel on Market and Third Streets in 1868. PHOTOGRAPH COURTESY OF THE SAN FRANCISCO HISTORY CENTER, SAN FRANCISCO PUBLIC LIBRARY.

of these ads were for girls working on their own, while others were for madams, like the one for "Miss Belle Raymond and assistants, parlor 2; massage."[6] The aptly named Nucleus Hotel at the corner of Market and Third Streets was a hub of such activity.

This devious advertising by San Francisco prostitutes and madams demonstrates how persistent these women were in pursuing their occupations and keeping them viable. By 1910, it was reported that San Francisco had nearly 6,000 prostitutes out of its 416,000 souls.[7] Per capita, this meant that San Francisco had about 1,442 prostitutes per 100,000 residents. This was nearly double the ratio of much larger Chicago (2 million residents at the time), which had 15,000 prostitutes, or about 750 per 100,000.[8]

CATHERINE REITER

It was a cold November night in 1867 when a pair of twenty-year-old sailors arrived at Catherine's Sacramento Street brothel. Once inside, she offered them wine and they settled in the parlor before they selected their female of choice. The evening was just like any other until the sailors prepared to leave her establishment. Upon their departure, she told them to hand over $5 for the wine she offered them. They took offense; they had assumed the wine was free, so they refused to pay. When they tried to leave, Catherine and one of her girls, Nellie, blocked them from leaving. Catherine's husband, Henry, was also nearby. Unfortunately for the women, Frank Lines, second mate of the steamship the *Granite State*, was carrying a small caliber Smith & Wesson. He fired two shots.

Initial reports stated that Catherine was hit with one ball that passed through her cheek and knocked out two of her teeth. The other bullet lodged into the neck of poor Nellie, who would share Catherine's plight of nasty scars earned over a single bottle of wine. Upon their arrest, Lines and his fellow sailor George Smith were outraged. Lines claimed he acted in self-defense and said the women were beating him about the face with tumblers and other items. He did have many cuts around his face, and he may have even been telling the truth, but the police didn't buy it.

A few days later, Dr. Murphy, who was taking care of the women, reported that Nellie indeed would recover. Because she had choked and swallowed much of the blood that poured into her throat, she also swallowed the bullet that entered her neck. The doctor concluded, ". . . it is not therefore likely to trouble her much more." Catherine, on the other hand, was worse than was first reported. The bullet left a large gash in her cheek and lodged under her jaw, making it too risky to remove. Henry was also grazed in the shooting affray.[9] In early December 1867, Frank Lines was charged with assault with a deadly weapon for shooting at Henry, and just before Christmas, he was charged for assault with intent to commit murder against Catherine.[10] Lines was also accompanied by George Smith, who was convicted of petty larceny for stealing jewelry from Catherine's brothel.[11]

Catherine was a native of Württemberg, Germany, born around 1838 into unknown circumstances. It's not known when she arrived in America, but she made her way to the Golden State and began operating as a madam as early as 1867. While she was operating her establishment, her husband Henry was running a saloon at the southwest corner of Sacramento and Brooklyn Streets. Henry was about five years older than Catherine, and by 1867, reports show they were calling themselves husband and wife, although there are no records that show when, and if, they truly were married. Henry was born in Hesse-Darmstadt, Germany, and became a naturalized U.S. citizen on October 6, 1852, in Albany, New York. Catherine's husband was a hustler and swindler and moved around San Francisco in various businesses and schemes. Henry would become notorious for his money-making schemes, and in December 1868, one of them caught up with him. John Pforr was the president of the Germania Savings and Building Union when he had Henry arrested for obtaining money under false pretenses and sued him for $5,000 in damages.[12]

On January 22, 1869, Henry and "wife" set sail for New York aboard the Pacific SS *Constitution*, passing through Aspinwall (today's Colón), Panama.[13] Once in Panama, Henry, along with Catherine—traveling as "Charlotte"—boarded the SS *Henry Chauncey* and arrived in New York on February 13, 1869.[14] It appears that she and Henry traveled to New York to procure some new girls for her Chinatown tenement brothel in San Francisco's Sixth Ward. The following year, her girls included seventeen-year-old Rosa Keipar and twenty-year-old June Hornstein from Prussia, twenty-year-old Poland native Selma Kamauski, twenty-year-old Kelly Bowman and twenty-four-year-old Fanny Smith from New York, a twenty-one-year-old French maiden named Catherine DeMouplas, and twenty-three-year-old Cassy Gilman of Massachusetts.

Henry kept busy in the Alaska Saloon at the northwest corner of Bush and Kearny Streets. While the U.S. Census showed only a tenement building for Catherine's address, Henry lived at 835 Sacramento Street, which was in the Sixth Ward and was likely her address as well. She and Henry were doing well if their wealth was measured in real estate. Catherine claimed her real estate holdings were valued at

$2,000 and her personal property at $2,500. Henry's personal property was valued at $1,000.

In February 1870, Henry became involved in a scheme to visit Japan and bring back the best entertainers that could be procured. He and partner J. S. Susenbeth, who lived at 523 Kearny, sold another Kearny Street resident, distiller P. Walfinger, on their scheme. Henry claimed he would put up two-thirds of the $10,000 and Walfinger was to supply the remainder, entrusting it to Henry. In late September, Walfinger realized he'd been duped when Henry failed to furnish the funds. He took Henry and Susenbeth to court to get his money back and was awarded $1,000.[15] A year later, Henry found himself the subject of a story in the *San Francisco Chronicle* entitled, "The Social Evil." The story unveiled how a young woman named Cora Lee was procured by Henry when he made another trip to New York in search of new girls for Catherine's brothel.

When Cora arrived at her new residence on Sacramento Street, she found beautiful dresses, hats, and more to please her clients. She was young but not new to the business. It wasn't long before she tired of life at Catherine's place and decided to look for work somewhere else. Fearing the wrath of Catherine and Henry, she quietly fled, leaving everything behind. She later sent a friend to retrieve her items, but Catherine and Henry refused to give her anything. The Reiters claimed the clothes were given to Cora to use nightly for the sole use of entertaining. In early January, Henry took Cora to court, but the case was promptly dismissed and the judge reportedly was disgusted with Henry for trying to extort money from girls by having them arrested.

The trouble between Henry and Cora was far from over. A month later, Henry found himself in the Fifteenth Judicial District Court, defending himself against Cora, but this time Henry had Cora arrested for a second time on grand larceny charges for taking her clothes. The charge was dismissed against Cora; the court opined that the clothes she took were her own. Henry then sued Cora to try and get the dresses back, but he lost again. That's when Cora countersued Henry for $5,000 to recover damages for her false imprisonment. When he appeared at the court hearing, Catherine accompanied him. Cora's attorney, W. E. Turner, incurred the wrath of the Reiters as a result of the remarks he made during the case, and after the court was adjourned that evening, both Henry and Catherine physically attacked Turner. Although he wasn't hurt, Turner was frightened by the angry couple, who were promptly arrested by the sheriff. The jury rendered a decision in favor of Cora and she was awarded $1,500.[16] Henry just couldn't let it go, and in early October he filed another motion against Cora, but Judge John Dwinelle denied him, yet again. Cora felt she had earned the clothes and filed an action with the court to have them returned to her. Judge Stanley was outraged that such a case was even brought to his court. The *Chronicle* reported the judge's anger and noted that he

> gave a verdict in favor of the plaintiff, stating that although the question before him was one that was a disgrace to the morality of San Francisco, nevertheless as soon as the plaintiff fulfilled her part in the contract by giving herself up to the vicious courses desired by her employer, if even for a shorter time that she had actually done, the clothes having been delivered to her became hers by right, and therefore they must be returned at once. That such a case as this should be brought up to our law courts is a matter of great surprise. One would imagine that keepers of such places as this one on Sacramento Street would wish their mode of living be kept secret from the general public; but they appear entirely lost to even the most outward semblance of decency. Throughout the whole proceeding Reiter sat in the court with the most unblushing effrontery, and apparently seemed to glory in his position.[17]

Around 1876, Catherine's brothel had moved to 828 Stockton Street, where clients could choose among twenty-three-year-old Minnie Schmidt and her nineteen-year-old sister Martha Schmidt, both from Germany; Ida Grant, twenty-two, from Frankfurt, Germany; twenty-two-year-old Lizzie Half of Pennsylvania; and Carrie Wells, an eighteen-year-old native of California. While Catherine was managing her brothel, Henry was running another saloon, bouncing from

309 Pine to 213 Pine, and then to 215 Pine. Henry's scheming got him into trouble once again, when he was sued in early 1880 by James J. Pettigrew over an accounting issue, and was forced by the courts to remand $3,802.72.[18] It appears that by June 1880, a "married" Henry was living in the Fifth Ward by himself and operating a saloon. In 1882, Henry again moved his business, this time to the southwest corner of Commercial and East at 315–317 East. His new residential address was 5 Market Street, and in 1883 he took a partner by the name of Fred Cranz; they ran a liquor store at 315 East.

Catherine was operating her brothel at a building at the corner of Pine and Kearny, where, interestingly, "prostitutes and lawyers shared the second floor." One of her girls, Ida Bailey, got drunk, so Catherine kicked her out and retained her expensive clothing as compensation. But in January 1883, Ida filed a suit against Catherine because she felt she had earned the $300 worth of clothes.[19] The paper reported there were enough clothes to fill a millinery store,[20] including piles of velvet and silk dresses and a large stock of "snowy garments." When asked if she knew Catherine, Ida stood and said dramatically, "Yes, and to my sorrow." She moved her arms with such animation that she almost slapped the judge. Fellow prostitutes Cora Birch and Lizzie McConnell testified in her support,[21] and on April 13, the judge awarded Ida $75 in damages, her clothes returned, and court costs.[22] Ida eventually moved to San Diego, where she became her own madam (see Chapter Six).

Louisa Seymour was a young brunette residing in Catherine's mansion in April 1884. A writ of habeas corpus was filed stating Louisa was being held against her will at Catherine's place. It was reported that Louisa was walking along Dupont Street when she was abducted and shoved into a waiting hack. When Catherine and Louisa appeared in court, they both testified that Louisa was, in fact, living under Catherine's roof of her own free will. Louisa stated she was pleased with her madam and was an inmate of the house of her own volition. The judge responded, "You are free to roam the broad American continent." Louisa stated she was nineteen, but the paper reported that "she does not appear to have seen more than fifteen summers. Throwing a contemptuous glance at the spectators, she walked out of the courtroom under the maternal eye of the madam."[23]

In September 1885, Catherine was called to testify in a similar case regarding a young woman named Emma Gass. The defendant was twenty-six-year-old Charles Wadleigh, who the *Daily Alta* called a sorry-looking specimen of the "lover" class for enticing the young fifteen-year-old Emma into a life of prostitution. Catherine took the stand and stated that Wadleigh had brought Miss Gass to her house on the 27th of August and procured a room for her. Emma told Catherine that she was an orphan, was eighteen years of age, and came from Santa Cruz, California. A witness testified that the couple had visited other houses of ill fame before going to Catherine's establishment.

After that witness testified, a motion was made to have the case dismissed on the grounds that "there was no proof that the girl had been enticed into leading a life of shame. Defendant's counsel claimed that the only fact proven was that five-foot, eight-inch Wadleigh had entered a house of ill fame in company with the young girl."[24] The motion was denied, however, and Emma was called as a witness for the defense. When Emma first took the stand, the apparently scared fifteen-year-old burst into tears and refused to testify. After a few soothing words of advice from the court, she regained her composure. She went on to testify that Wadleigh had not put her in Catherine's house, that she had gone there of her own accord, and that Wadleigh had gone with her only as far as the front door. At that point in her testimony, she became bold and brazen, and declared she had never received any visitors or made any money in the house. She did admit, however, that she had been with Wadleigh ever since she left home. Catherine was called in rebuttal to testify that Emma had received gentlemen visitors, and one of them had given her a present. In mid-December, a whimpering and quivering Wadleigh stood before Judge Murphy. Convicted of a felony, he began his five-year sentence at Folsom State Prison on December 15, 1885. The judge said he only regretted that the sentence was so short because he knew Wadleigh's reputation in Oakland and that Emma wasn't his first victim.[25]

It's not known when Catherine and Henry split, but a newspaper account claims he was married three times. By 1886, Henry had moved and was living at 325½ Bush Street at a rooming house run by Mrs. Rose Unfried, and in 1887, Mrs. C. Reiter was running a saloon back at her old brothel address of 835 Sacramento Street. At this point, it seems that he and Catherine had parted ways. By 1888, Henry had lost his saloon and was a bartender for George Lang at Lang & Co. on First Street. He was living in a room at 522 Howard and then at 569 Howard Street. Henry may have moved because he was sued for $50 in past due rent by Nelson C. Walton on September 11, 1889.[26] In 1890, Henry was back to being a saloonkeeper, but he had moved to 19 Minna Street. Henry died on July 28, 1890, in San Francisco, at the age of fifty-seven years, three months, and three days.

A few months after Henry died, Catherine sued Joseph Rothschild, who was the executor of Hannah Rothschild's will. Catherine wanted $500 that she claimed she had loaned to the sixty-two-year-old Hannah in 1889 before her death and was never repaid.[27] After this involvement with the courts, Catherine's tawdry life disappears from the records. In the 1890s, Catherine's notorious brothel at 828 Sacramento Street was turned into a Chinese hospital.

Cora Lee

Cora Lee was a determined black girl who began her career in the employ of Catherine Reiter in the late 1860s in San Francisco. After leaving and winning a case against her former employers, Cora took her elegant Victorian dresses and became a madam with her own operation on Dupont Street by November 1871.

Her establishment was said to be a disgrace to the community where young girls, from age ten to eighteen, could be procured. When police raided her brothel, they discovered both white and black girls in her employ. When officers entered the Dupont Street house, they found a fourteen-year-old girl named Cora Brittan cowering under the piano. She would later testify that her madam took half of their profits, which Cora Lee corroborated when she later took the stand.[28] Cora was quite angry when they raided her brothel and she cursed at the officers. So, on top of her misdemeanor charge for keeping a house of ill fame, she was slapped with a charge of using violent language against Chief Crowley. She was brought before a judge to explain herself for that charge, in addition to facing a trial. After several hours of deliberation, the jury returned a guilty verdict and the judge offered her a choice between a $200 fine or a sentence of 100 days in jail. Like most madams of her day, she promptly paid the fine but also agreed to quit the business and leave the neighborhood.[29]

A month later, Cora was again in full operation at her house on Dupont Street. Chief Crowley, with the earlier verbal assault still fresh, instructed his men to rescue any underage girls or women who did not wish to remain in a house of ill fame. If found, they were to be taken into custody and then to City Hall where their fate would be decided.

In 1872, Cora once again visited the local justice system because of her foul mouth. For reasons unknown, Cora burst into the home of Carrie Brown, who was entertaining Frank Merrifield, and the two women began cursing at each other. Carrie Brown charged Cora with calling her vile names and intruding on her property. The *San Francisco Chronicle* called her a "profane courtesan." Carrie Brown stated, "Miss Lee came in a-rushing and a-tearing and a-pitching" and began to assault Merrifield. Brown claimed Merrifield was a friend of hers and the two were merely sitting in her apartment when the incident occurred. In the end, Cora Lee and Merrifield were fined $30 each for vulgar language—her for using it in general and him for using it against Cora.[30]

That is the last mention of Cora Lee of San Francisco in the historical record. Like so many madams, she simply vanished into the passing years.

MADAM APPEL

By 1870, forty-year-old madam Margaret Appel and her thirty-one-year-old husband Phillip were operating a luxurious mansion at 826–828 Sacramento Street, between Dupont and Stockton Streets. The section where the building stood contained many brothels within or on the border of Chinatown. It was also the same mansion that Catherine Reiter moved into after Appel left around 1876. Interestingly, a Louis Appel, from Hanover, Germany, was a bartender right next door to the Reiters in 1870. The couple were both from Hesse-Darmstadt, Germany, and had done well in the sex trade, including the accumulation of real estate valued at $10,000 and personal assets worth $2,500.[31] Oddly enough, the census lists Phillip as keeping a brothel, while Margaret is "keeping house." Also living with them were their four-year-old daughter, four prostitutes, and two Chinese domestic servants. The working girls were Louisa Walter, aged twenty-four, from Prussia; Maria Ryne, eighteen, from Mecklenburg, New York; Lena Stein, twenty, from New York; and Hetty Warren, twenty, from Berlin, Germany. Their young daughter was also named Lena and was born in Hesse-Darmstadt, Germany, in 1866.

In October 1871, Margaret was fined $10 for shouting "billingsgate" at another woman.[32] (This was the newspaper's euphemism for saying she was using coarse language. From as early as the Roman occupation, Billingsgate was a fish market in London, renowned for the vulgar language of its fishmongers. By the 1650s, the name was well in use as a synonym for swearing.) To keep her business running, Margaret and many other madams were forced to offer their girls for free to two corrupt police officers named Rogers and Lindheimer. When they made their rounds in the district and knocked on doors, the madams knew they had to pay with their girls and free champagne, wine, and food. Despite these in-kind services, the cops often arrested them anyway. In 1874, the law finally caught up with the lawmen, and Rogers and Lindheimer were put on trial. Madam after madam was called to testify against them, including Madam Appel.

Her competition, a madam named Miss Camille, testified, "[I] know Officers Rogers and Lindheimer; Lindheimer arrested me the first time on Sacramento Street; the second time I was arrested by Rogers, who sent someone to me; I moved away from there because I saw them go to Mrs. Apel [*sic*], who was jealous of me; I moved to Waverly Place. . . ." Before she moved, Margaret and Camille had some raucous incidents. Camille also testified, "I know Mrs. Apel [*sic*]; she came once to my window and insulted me; the officers know her perfectly; Mrs. Apel [*sic*] came to me and made a threat to me that if I did not put my head in the window I would be arrested; I was arrested five minutes afterward; I whistled three times for a policeman when she insulted me; Rogers and Lindheimer came and told me to dress myself; I was charged with soliciting prostitution, and put up five dollars bail."[33]

Despite her fine, Madam Appel continued her tradition of holding quarterly birthday parties for herself. They began at midnight with a brass band belting out tunes that flowed down to Kearny Street. The paper wrote, "Madam Appel has three or four birthdays in every year for the purpose of affording her female slaves opportunities to lavish their sinful earnings in presents for her."[34]

Madam Appel, like other madams, procured some of her girls from the East, but she mostly worked with girls from her native country. In late January 1876, she was expecting two new girls, one of them possibly named Clara Schultz. But Appel discovered they were traveling by overland train with Sam Rosenblatt, a notorious jewel thief who was wanted by the authorities, so she asked Detective Rogers to ensure the girls' delivery to her. When eighteen-year-old German Clara Schultz arrived at Castle Garden in New York (America's first official immigration center), a procuress approached her and told her she could get her a job as a servant in San Francisco and her passage would be paid. She agreed, but when she arrived at Madam Appel's mansion, she realized she was in a house of prostitution and she was not going to be the kind servant she had expected. She made numerous attempts to leave, but Madam Appel restrained her and was told she had to stay until she paid back her passage. Eventually, Appel tired of dealing with Clara, so she turned her over to Madam Green, who lived across the street, for $250. A visitor to the house heard her story and reported it to the chief of police, who then sent Officer Seybold to investigate. Seybold visited the house and told the girl she was free to leave, which she joyfully did.[35] An application for an arrest warrant was made out for Appel, but the judge refused to sign it, citing that no prosecution could stand under the law because there was nothing to prove that Clara had been restrained.[36]

In August 1878, Margaret Appel tried to take custody of her two minor nieces, Tallie and Lulu, who preferred to stay with her rather than their parents, the Mays. When the hearing took place at probate court, the secretary of the Society for the Prevention of Cruelty to Children, Nathaniel Hunter, recommended they be placed in his custody. Hunter asked to be the girls' guardian and stated that neither the girls' parents nor their aunt should have custody.[37] Two days later, Judge Milton

Myrick ruled in favor of Nathaniel Hunter, and neither the parents nor Margaret Appel got custody. Tallie and Lulu told the judge they felt their parents were improper and could not take care of them.[38]

Margaret's husband Phillip ran a "liquor saloon" at 826–828 Sacramento Street from 1874 to 1876, but two years later he moved and was living at 911 Clay Street. It appears that Phillip and Margaret were no longer together by 1880, and Phillip was out of the saloon business and working as a wheelwright and living at the Hotel Rhein at 909 Kearny. He claimed he was single, and by 1903 he was back in the red-light area at 125 Eddy Street.

By early 1885, Margaret's then nineteen-year-old daughter Lena had an unclaimed letter waiting for her at the post office, so it appears she may have moved from San Francisco. Margaret silently faded into history.

HATTIE A. WELLS

Hattie Wells's claim to fame is that she was likely the madam who employed lawman Wyatt Earp's last wife, Josephine Sarah Marcus, who, for a brief time, worked as a prostitute. Hattie had what people called a high-end establishment with a beautiful house, gorgeous girls, and luxurious clothing. Hattie A. Wells was born around 1835 in New York. Nothing is known about her childhood, but she made her way to California by 1860.

Hattie was one of five girls in their twenties living with a fifty-six-year-old woman named Mary Dunham in the Sixth Ward, which was notorious for brothels. None of the women living there had an occupation listed except for the alleged "house keeper." It's interesting to note that the head of the household at their residence was one Elizabeth Blain, aged twenty-seven, who claimed real estate valued at $3,500 and personal assets of $2,500. Next was Mary Blain, aged twenty-nine, whose real estate assets were valued at $8,000 and personal assets at $1,000. The housekeeper had no assets of note, and Hattie and the other girl, Cath Williams, each had personal assets of $1,500.[39]

By 1867, Hattie had become a madam and established herself in a gilded mansion on Waverly Place. This alley between Dupont and Stockton Streets was notorious for its bold vice, running just outside the Barbary Coast. Hattie's place was remarkable compared to most of the cribs that filled the area. Many were nothing more than ramshackle, dilapidated, low-frame buildings. The same was true of the soiled doves, who were just that. These women were vice-worn, sickly, or desperate. They were abundantly painted, powdered, and gaudily attired in an attempt to attract customers. In contrast, Hattie's girls were a welcome change for those who wanted a more refined experience. Her girls wore the latest fashions and lived in luxurious style, but it came with a price. While this life appeared glamorous to many young girls, their life was hard, and they endured untold perversions.

Hattie ensured that her clients and her girls experienced all the luxury that life could offer. This was good for employee morale, and it drew in a wealthier class of clientele. While she employed many girls at her place, only the names of Irish native Minnie Bell, Maud Duval, and "a colored woman named Aunty Bess" are known. During the day, Hattie's place was a simple, ordinary house, and the local streets were quiet and seemed almost desolate. But when the sun sank below the horizon, the lights inside the buildings began to illuminate the darkness along Waverly Place.[40] Doors and windows were thrown open so passersby could see the women inside sporting their glamorous costumes. Hattie's place was easily recognizable because of the red light that shone from the transom and the name "Wells" upon it. Upon entering her tony mansion, customers walked into the drawing room, which was a double apartment enclosed with folding doors. The walls were ornately papered, the floor covered with plush carpets, and the ceilings were adorned with shimmering crystal chandeliers. A Chickering piano sat in the corner where a German musician tinkled the ivories to entertain the customers. An adjoining section housed a card room where the girls waited for clients. The girls' rooms were also elegantly decorated, and when they were not entertaining, they relaxed in flowing robes with long trains, white satin boots with rosettes, diamond earrings, and glittering rings on their fingers.[41]

Hattie's bagnio was at the front and center of attention in December 1869 when Minnie Bell ran off with a well-to-do married whiskey rectifier named George Parker. It was a sensational story that began when twenty-eight-year-old Parker became infatuated with Minnie.

Minnie's friend and coworker Maud had introduced them on the way back from the state fair in September. Minnie didn't take to Parker right way, but he did to her—despite him having an attractive, loving, and devoted wife of eight years waiting for him at the Occidental Hotel where they lived. Minnie was a pretty young blonde who had been hurt in the past by an actor and vowed to never love again, but Parker wore her down. By October, they were inseparable, and by December, they had fled California to Australia, where his family lived. It was later learned that he stole about $4,000 from his partners at the liquor business. Soon after, his wife went after George and Minnie.[42] The thrill of the story faded away until seventeen years later, when all the sordid details would be learned.

With Minnie gone, Hattie brought in some new girls. She housed New Yorker Julia Clement, who was thirty, somewhat old for a prostitute. Most of Julia's brothel sisters were also from New York and included the twenty-year-old Hattie Seymour, nineteen-year-old Molly Clark, twenty-one-year-old Eva Lamont, and seventeen-year-old Minna Lee, a California native. Hattie also employed fifty-year-old Maria Green as a domestic servant and Allen Bissel as her porter. Unfortunately, not long after she got her girls settled and business was moving along, Hattie was assaulted by a man named Dave McCarthy. In October 1870, she took him to court for punching her in the eye. The judge dismissed the case, but McCarthy still had to pay a fine.[43]

Hattie didn't let a black eye slow her down, and her business was doing well. Three years later, on February 28, 1873, she moved from 3 Waverly Place and had her furnishings loaded onto an express wagon. She soon realized that she was missing expensive bed linens and believed they had fallen off the wagon. She placed a newspaper ad asking for their return and noted they could likely be found on Dupont Street between Bush and Market Streets (a distance of four blocks). She also offered a reward when they were returned to her.[44] Whether she ever got them back is unknown.

In the early 1870s, Hattie made repeated trips to Prescott, Arizona, while she was setting up her new location. The October 20, 1874, issue of Prescott's *Weekly Arizona Miner* (which underwent several name changes and mergers through the years) carried the following item: "Named passengers who left Wickenberg this morning en route to Prescott from San Francisco: Miss Hattie Wells, Miss Ella Howard, Miss Saddie [sic] Mansfield [Josephine Marcus Earp's nom de guerre], Miss Minnie Alice and Mrs. Julia Burton, a servant."

Four years later, in 1878, Hattie was shuffling her girls between California and Arizona, and in August, she took Willey Beatty, who was likely a new girl, to California. Then on September 13, the two unnamed women, along with J. Clark and F. Gray, arrived in Prescott on a stagecoach from California. Hattie seems to have settled in by 1879, and in 1880, the *Arizona Weekly Miner* reported that she had returned by stage in early January, after having been in the southern part of the territory.[45]

When Hattie left for Prescott, Aunty Bess did not go with her, instead staying in San Francisco in rooms on Broadway, and then moving to Vallejo. It was rumored that Aunty Bess was keeping someone in the rooms on Broadway, but no one had ever seen anyone other than Aunty Bess come and go. Some said they could see a frail, skeletal figure passing by the windows inside. For two years, Aunty Bess cared for this unknown, frail creature, and then the invalid finally succumbed to consumption in November 1887. Aunty Bess had the woman placed in a redwood box coffin and city officials took her to be placed in a pauper's grave at the City Cemetery. No longer needing to hide the truth, Aunty Bess divulged the end to Minnie Bell's escapades that began in 1869.

She revealed that Minnie and George were pursued by his wife from Auckland, New Zealand, to Sydney, Melbourne, and other Australian locations. They next headed to London with the hope of losing Mrs. Parker, which they did for ten years. In the end, George felt guilty about leaving his wife, and, with the help of friends and family, he went back to her. To appease Minnie, he gave her £500 and ended their relationship. Minnie returned to the trade she knew, this time in London. She earned some money, but her income could not keep up with her expenses. She managed to save enough to book passage back to San Francisco, where Aunty Bess cared for her until she died, likely in her forties.[46]

After Hattie Wells moved to Prescott, Arizona, her trail went cold.

AH TOY, AKA CHINA MARY OF ALVISO

The beautiful Cantonese immigrant Ah Toy (also spelled Atoy in some sources) is known to history as San Francisco's first Chinese madam. She was born in May 1828 in Canton, China, and she grew to be a tall, slender woman who was strangely alluring, with laughing eyes. She arrived in San Francisco in 1849 at the beginning of the gold rush. At twenty-one, she began her life as a prostitute in a shanty off Clay Street just above Kearny, in what would later become Chinatown. It was said that the lines outside her shanty were a block long because of her popularity and "peeping ability" (posing for peep shows).

Also in 1849, Ah Toy was first brought to an American court of law when a man from Hong Kong claimed she was his wife. He sent a letter stating he was her legal husband and wanted her returned to him. She told the judge she was *Miss* Ah Toy and had left Canton, via Hong Kong, to better her life's situation. The judge allowed her request to stay in America, but that would not be the end of it.

In 1850, Toy was one of only a handful of Chinese or "celestial" women in San Francisco, in contrast to the large population of Chinese men. Frank Soule lived in and wrote about San Francisco in the 1850s and recalled Ah Toy. He said everyone knew "Miss or Mrs. Atoy" and that she was an infamous woman who was also known as the laughingstock of the emerging Chinatown. The area then was on Dupont Street, with a portion of Pacific and other cross streets. He also laid blame on her for the arrival of scores of other Chinese women brought into the prostitution trade. He claimed her letters home encouraged young women to come to San Francisco since it was such a delightful spot. Soule wrote of them, ". . . they are the most indecent and shameless part of the population, without dwelling more particularly upon their manners and customs."[47]

Despite Soule's comments, Toy remained popular with the men in San Francisco, but she was quite upset when she discovered that she was being duped out of her fees. The tall courtesan appeared in court, at her own request, to file charges. She dressed in an apricot satin jacket and willowy green pantaloons. Her feet were bound, which was a Chinese tradition, and her dark silk hair was piled upon her head in a chignon. Her pencil-thin jet-black eyebrows were a stark

A bagnio in San Francisco's Chinatown, 1870. PHOTOGRAPH COURTESY OF THE SAN FRANCISCO HISTORY CENTER, SAN FRANCISCO PUBLIC LIBRARY.

contrast to her powdery white skin. Given the nature of the case and the prejudices of the time, it's not surprising that people in the courtroom found her appearance and broken English amusing. The judge asked her why the miners off the boats from Sacramento raced to her shanty. Everyone knew why, but her exact answer was not recorded. The paper of the day paraphrased her response as, "they came to gaze upon the countenance of the charming Ah Toy." Whatever her true answer was, it tickled those in the courtroom, and everyone roared.

When they got down to the details of her case, she told the judge that she charged each of her customers one ounce of gold (about $16), which she weighed out on her own scales in her room. It was over this payment that she was filing her complaint. She told the judge that some of the men were giving her brass filings in place of gold. The judge asked her for proof, so she went home, got some of the brass, and brought it to the judge. Because Toy could not tell exactly who gave her the brass versus the gold, the case was dismissed. It was her statement, and the newspaper's clean version of what was said, that led to the belief that Ah Toy was the first woman to start peep shows.

By 1850, Toy was no longer charging customers to gaze upon her. She had become a madam. She hired five Chinese girls to work for her and opened a large brick lodging house off Clay in an alley at 34–36 Pike Street (later changed to Waverly Place). Some of her notorious neighbors were madams Clara Hastings and Belle Cora. Toy, like her male counterparts, began importing young Chinese girls for prostitution. A year later, on a cool March day, Ah Toy was forced to deal yet again with a man claiming to be her husband back in Hong Kong. A letter had been received by Judge Woodworth with a renewed request to return her home. Her husband, Atchoung, claimed the twenty-four-year-old had been living in San Francisco in a "free and easy style," much to his dismay. Atchoung conferred with church authorities in Hong Kong and they sent an order for her return. They also sent the funds to cover her journey and appealed to the authorities to return her so she could perform her wifely duties. Although the authorities had refused before, Atchoung asked that they not interfere this time.[48] Two days later, Chinese residents of the city assembled in the Recorder's Office to witness the proceedings against Toy. A "Chinaman" named Apung was duly sworn and testified that he was a resident of Canton and knew Toy for about four months. During that time, he learned that she was twenty-four, unmarried, and came from Canton where her father had died and her mother still lived. He also stated that she came to America for the purpose of bettering her condition and she was anxious to make California her home and not return to China. Apung claimed there was a plot by three Chinamen in town who wanted to kidnap Toy. Arrests were sworn out for Norman

Assing, Leikid, and Chidock, because Apung swore that these men told Toy if she did not go to China with them, then they would kill her. He also stated that both Leikid and Chidock wanted to marry Toy themselves, but when she refused, they had decided they wanted her out of the country. The judge ordered bonds of $2,000 to keep the peace until a decision was made. Fifteen Chinamen quickly put up the money for the defendants.[49] The case did not go in Toy's favor, and a month later she and Apung were referred to as heretics and deserving of nothing less than "brimstone and red-hot pinchers."[50] Within two months of her case, a marriage announcement appeared in the May 22 *Daily Alta California* stating that Henry Conrad had married the well-known "Achoi" from Hong Kong on May 16 in Sonoma. It's not known what happened to Henry Conrad, but there's no trace in the historical record that he was in San Francisco with Ah Toy.

Despite her alleged marriage, Toy ran her crib off Clay Street, which was the scene of frequent fights and assaults. In May, John Roberts and A. Brown were arrested for assault committed on a Chinaman, and then in November, Robert Nelson was arrested, along with China Jim. According to reports, a knife-wielding China Jim had appeared at Toy's brothel and called Nelson out for a fight. China Jim ended up worse for the fight, but both were fined for disturbing the peace.[51] As a result of the fights taking place at Toy's establishment on Clay, which was opposite the post office, neighbors complained. The authorities charged her with keeping a disorderly house, and the newspaper called the girls inside "Chinese curiosities" who constantly caused a crowd to form, and fights often ensued because of their presence. A week later, the charges were dropped because Toy reportedly had "removed herself."[52]

Yet Toy had, in fact, not left. A month later, she called great attention to herself when she ran "screeching" down the street (on bound feet, no less) after a thief named Lewis Ottinger. She chased him through the plaza, and when she finally caught him, she horse-collared Ottinger. She then escorted him to the police station to settle the matter. She told the police that he had stolen a diamond breast pin worth $300 from her while "visiting and taking a drink" at her place.[53] A few days later and halfway to the New Year, Toy appeared in court with her usual flair to testify about the matter. The young and beautiful Toy arrived with rouge-colored cheeks, a bonnet, and an orange shawl. When an interpreter for her Chinese-speaking witness was excused because the court didn't think his English was good enough, Toy accused the court of stalling her case. Her protest began in a musical voice but then escalated to a pitch that frightened even the dour recorder, who nonetheless dutifully transcribed Toy's outburst, "You like tief man—you like stealy you pin? You very bad-man. Dat man stealy my pin—he ought be hang!" The court took a recess and sent for another interpreter while Toy berated Colonel James, who was Ottinger's attorney. She told him, "You thinkee dat man teefy 'cause he give you money." She then went on to assail all lawyers and their shady practices. The court adjourned to determine the outcome. The following day, Toy's diamond pin showed up at a local jeweler's shop where a man was trying to sell it. He explained that he received it from a man who found it. They located that man, who in turn, identified Lewis Ottinger as the one who gave him the pin. Ottinger was then charged with grand larceny.[54]

In 1852, Toy's diamond pin resurfaced in another crime, but this time it was her own doing. In February that year, she loaned her old pal, John Chinaman, Esquire, the diamond pin and a gold watch to polish his image. When she worried that he would run off, like her other beau had done, she had him arrested. Because there were no felonious intentions, the charge was dismissed.[55]

A traveler by the name of Alexander Holinski published a book in French about traveling to California, in which he recalled his impression of the lovely Ah Toy. He wrote:

The only Chinese girl I knew in San Francisco was very popular, not among her fellow citizens who do not often see her, but among Americans who sit near her door from morning to night. At her home, she appears dressed with her national costume, in the streets she is dressed as a European girl. She is not beautiful but she is prickly. But I heard that having tiny feet is an aristocratic privilege resulting from art and torture. Miss Atoy, who probably was a humble boatwoman in Canton or Hong Kong, doesn't have long legs like North girls and she is not pretty as the Andalusian or Limanian girls [from Lima]. The Chinese were shocked by the coquetries that this flower girl shows at her window or door. Lately [the] Chinese sent a delegation to the vigilance committee to ask them to stop her by exiling her or by any other punishment which would reprimand the pranks of this kind creature. Needless to say that the complaint was not able to be considered because the committee established against the thieves, the arsonists and the murderers would have too much to do to deal with insignificant things. It was said to scrupulous Chinese that it was impossible to make an exception for miss Atoy as San Francisco Police tolerate the same for American, French, German and Spanish women. The delegation, although disappointed withdrew the complaint, surprised by the same fairness of Barbarian's court towards thousands of women at least from the city or women coming from other lands.[56]

Since the police didn't bother Toy, her business flourished, and by 1854, Toy was not only housing her girls but also a commercial flour merchant named Henry Bush.[57] Her girls were subjected to the horrors that many working girls endured. Sadly, many had been sold to Toy by their parents. Toy paid $40 for each girl and $80 for their passage from China. Toy often functioned as a broker, reselling the girls to merchants and gamblers and netting anywhere from $1,000 to $1,500 per girl. In March 1855, Toy made plans to return to China. Wanting to sell her girls quickly, she reduced the price to $800. The girls had no say in the matter because they were considered nothing but chattel.[58] A few months later, "the celebrated Chinese courtesan," Ah Toy tried to kill herself by swallowing a large dose of opium. A doctor forced her to vomit the drug, sparing her life. According to the *Bulletin*, the once wealthy courtesan stated she was now in poverty and did not want to live.[59]

After this attempt to take her own life, Ah Toy went back to the life she knew and by some accounts headed to Sacramento. There are numerous accounts of *an* Ah Toy being arrested in Sacramento during the 1860s for enticing and other violations, but it cannot be confirmed it was *the* Ah Toy.

In October 1871, the *Daily Alta California* ran a notice that Ah Toy and One Ho were married in San Jose where they lived in the Chinese quarter until his death around 1903.[60] Toy then moved to a small house in the bay town of Alviso, where she earned the moniker China Mary of Alviso. She was known to yachting parties and fishermen alike because she sold clams to earn a living. She lived with her brother-in-law, Chinese Louis.

Ah Toy died on February 1, 1928, just three months shy of her one hundredth birthday. She is buried in the Oak Hill Cemetery in San Jose in the Chinese section, tier ten, grave twenty-seven.[61]

TERESA SUSAN "TESSIE" DONOHUE-WALL-DAROUX

A blonde, Irish lass by the name of Teresa "Tessie" Susan Donohue would be remembered as one of the most celebrated madams of her day. She was born to John and Sarah into an average Irish family who lived in the Mission District, or "South 'o the slot," as it was called back then by the locals. John and Sarah welcomed their new baby girl into the world on May 26, 1869. Tessie and her siblings—William, Sarah, Joseph, Rosilla, and Isabelle "Bella"—lived on Miller's Place in 1880. Her father was a laborer and her mother was confined to the house due to illness. In 1884, Mr. M. M. Miller placed an attachment on their place for $40 and named Tessie's mother as the responsible party.[62] When Sarah Ferren-Donohue died in her mid-forties on September 21, 1885, Tessie and her siblings had to work to make ends meet. Childhood friends recalled Tessie talking about taking the veil to become a nun, but no one took her seriously.

Clearly never following up on her talk about being a nun, Tessie became pregnant, married Edward M. Wall on April 29, 1886, and began working as a maid. One of Tessie's greatest days occurred on August 21, 1886, when her first and only child, Joseph Lawrence Wall, was born.[63] Being the good Catholic girl that she was, she took him to St. Rose's Catholic Church, where he was baptized along with another boy named Joseph Lawrence McCarthy. Tessie became the McCarthy boy's godmother and Maria McCarthy became young Wall's god-mother.[64] If Tessie's greatest joy was the day her son was born, then the day of her worst sorrow was when he died a few months later. She was devastated and ended up alone when Edward deserted her.

Three years later, Tessie had established herself as a single, *Miss* Tessie Wall living at 928 Dolores Street. She stayed there for a while, but then moved and, as *Mrs*. Tessie Wall, was running a lodging house at 137 O'Farrell from 1897 to 1900. In January 1898, Tessie asked for a divorce from Edward on the grounds of desertion. Her divorce was granted late that same month.[65] Tessie, like most well-known mad-ams, kept moving around, and sometime in 1900, the newly divorced Tessie relocated her brothel to 211 O'Farrell. As Tessie's business grew, she began to accumulate wealth and gilded furniture, with which she decorated her homes. Tessie lived there with her twenty-two-year-old Japanese houseman named Choy Loi, along with Albert McKay, Cassie Harlow, and Gertrude Day. She once again packed up her an-tiques, golden mirrors, and everything else she had accumulated, and quickly moved and opened a new house called the Nelson Lodgings at 147 Powell Street. With all those luxurious items in her home, it was only a matter of time before someone succumbed to temp-tation. Two years after Tessie opened the Nelson, a laborer named Clyde Greenacre stole one of her expensive French clocks. When she discovered the clock missing, Tessie called for the police, who tracked down Greenacre and arrested him. He was later charged with petty larceny at the Central Station.[66] By 1904, Tessie ensured that she would be ready to call the police, or anyone else for that matter —she had a phone installed. (Residential telephones were relatively rare at the time. In 1900, there were only 600,000 telephones in the American Telegraph and Telephone system. By 1905, with a total U.S. population of nearly 85 million, the number of phones had risen to just 2.2 million.)

Tessie's audacity didn't stop with the décor in her home. She show-ered her girls with all the latest fashions. Not wanting to waste all that on just the customers who came to her door, she began a fashion show of sorts. She had her girls put on their new dresses and then boldly paraded the elegantly fashioned girls along Market Street on Saturday

The April 18, 1906, earthquake and subsequent fires reduced much of San Francisco to rubble. Here, buildings on Market Street smolder.
PHOTOGRAPH COURTESY OF THE LIBRARY OF CONGRESS, LC-USZ62-96789.

afternoons so everyone could see the "merchandise." Both men and women crowded the streets so they could see the latest couture.

Tessie, like everyone in San Francisco at the time, was taken completely by surprise when the city was rocked by a massive earthquake on the morning of April 18, 1906. She endured the earthquake, and then the fires that ensued, as residents watched their city turn into rubble and burnt debris. Tessie didn't let the disaster slow her down, and she went back into business shortly after the fire, living in the burnt district. There Tessie was watched and then raided by Captain John Mooney. Mooney was aware of Tessie's activities and placed six officers to stake out her brothel. Hers wasn't the only one being watched, and Mooney was set on obtaining evidence that Tessie and several others were operating houses of ill fame. Mooney had spoken out many times against the Board of Commissioners, who he felt weren't trying to suppress these businesses but were instead aiding them. When Mooney got close to making some arrests, he and his men were quickly taken off the beat and replaced with others. However, those men also disappeared rather quickly, and

Jeremiah F. Dinan, San Francisco chief of police, 1907. PHOTOGRAPH COURTESY OF THE
SAN FRANCISCO HISTORY CENTER, SAN FRANCISCO PUBLIC LIBRARY.

*Captain John Mooney of
the San Francisco Police.*
PHOTOGRAPH COURTESY OF THE
SAN FRANCISCO HISTORY CENTER,
SAN FRANCISCO PUBLIC LIBRARY.

when suspicion arose, Chief of Police Jeremiah F. Dinan claimed they were removed because of dangerous gas pipe work being done in the area. San Francisco had been a corrupt town before, but graft and skullduggery thrived in the chaotic aftermath of the big quake.

In December 1906, Dinan was indicted by a grand jury for perjury related to protecting brothels at 712 Pacific Street and 620 Jackson Street. Dinan said he did not shut down the houses because a local reverend, Father Terence Caraher, had no objection to their operation—the houses weren't in his parish. In fact, police records revealed, Father Caraher had previously lodged formal complaints with Dinan's police department. Signaling the severity of the charges against Dinan, Judge Murasky set a bond of $5,000 on each count of perjury and ordered him arrested on December 1. (The same grand jury also indicted San Francisco political boss Abe Ruef on charges of protecting the Pacific Street "resort" in exchange for payment from the brothel's owner. Ruef held all the strings controlling his "puppet," Mayor Eugene Schmitz, and was siphoning large sums of money from the efforts to rebuild the city, including the telephone, trolley, and gas systems. Ruef was also paying bribes to every member on the Board of Commissioners.) Dinan paid the bond and, for a time, continued as chief of police even under the cloud of the perjury charges.

Captain Mooney didn't relent, however, and in early 1907, he became convinced that Tessie's place needed to be closed, so he raided her house. On the day of the raid, Chief of Police Dinan told Mooney that Tessie was a poor woman who was just operating a lodging house to earn a living in a burnt neighborhood. Dinan told Mooney to "leave her alone," but Mooney later testified that Dinan told him to "protect her." Captain Mooney boldly told his chief that if he learned Tessie was operating a house of ill fame in his district, then he would raid her again. The very next day, March 5, 1907, the boundaries of Mooney's district were changed and Tessie's establishment was no longer within his control. Later, Mooney was accused of insubordination and stood before the Board of Commissioners. During the investigation, Chief Dinan accused Mooney of having relations with Tessie. Captain Mooney was angered and stated, "I refuse to be questioned by you here, but when this matter comes up before the proper tribunal I will answer all questions and I will put you where you belong."[67]

Mooney's threat apparently had some teeth. During Dinan's perjury trial, the chief was demoted to patrolman and replaced by "perhaps the only honest man in a corrupt city," William Biggy, who was sworn in as police chief in September 1907. Biggy had risen through the ranks in part because he had ably guarded Abe Ruef for more than a year during Ruef's corruption trial—all the other available jailers were on Ruef's payroll. Sadly, Biggy didn't last long. On November 13, 1908, one of Ruef's henchman, Morris Haas, on trial for extortion,

Officer William Biggy (left, facing camera) escorting Abe Ruef (center) during the graft trial in 1907. PHOTOGRAPH COURTESY OF THE CALIFORNIA STATE LIBRARY.

smuggled a handgun into the courtroom and shot Assistant District Attorney Francis Heney. The wound wasn't fatal, but Haas was found in his cell the next day, dead from a gunshot to the head. Guards found a single-shot Derringer in his shoe. The newspapers suggested it was suicide, but the circumstances were certainly suspicious. The papers also criticized Chief Biggy for negligence and called for his removal from office. The Citizens' League of Justice soon filed charges against Biggy for "gross incompetency" and dereliction of duty. The papers kept up a barrage of criticism. *The San Francisco Call* "was particularly active in the fight against Biggy and on [November 30] published a sensational story of a midnight escapade in a bawdy house in which the police chief was made to figure prominently."[68] That very evening, Chief Biggy boarded the police boat *Patrol* and motored north across the bay to Belvedere for a secret meeting with Police Commissioner Hugo Keil, apparently to tender his resignation. Keil counseled Biggy

The Patrol *police launch.* PHOTOGRAPH COURTESY OF THE SAN FRANCISCO HISTORY CENTER, SAN FRANCISCO PUBLIC LIBRARY.

Chief William Biggy. PHOTOGRAPH COURTESY OF THE SAN FRANCISCO HISTORY CENTER, SAN FRANCISCO PUBLIC LIBRARY.

to be patient, and they agreed to meet the next morning in Keil's office. Biggy boarded the *Patrol* to cross back to San Francisco, and the only other person on board, the pilot, Police Engineer William Murphy, guided the craft past Angel and Alcatraz Islands. But when the boat docked at the city pier, Biggy was nowhere to be found. Rumors circled—he had accidentally fallen overboard, he had jumped, he was murdered. Two weeks later, on December 14, Biggy's body was found in San Francisco Bay between the city and Yerba Buena Island. A watch in his pocket had stopped at 9:12, presumably on the night of November 30th. An autopsy found no signs of foul play. (According to *The Call*, three years later, on November 6, 1911, Engineer Murphy—suffering from alcoholism and haunted by the mystery of Biggy's death—was committed to Agnew State Hospital by the "lunacy commission.")

Tessie had moved out of the burnt district in 1907 to a better home at 664 Larkin Street. Tessie, along with Jessie Hayman, were two of the most well-known and respected madams in the city and were both living in the Tenderloin District—about five blocks apart from each other. One was just as ostentatious as the other, both treated their girls and clients well, and both wanted to be the top at her game. Tessie went back to parading her girls with their latest fashions; however, this time it wasn't on the street, but for a captive audience. The newly built Orpheum Theatre on Fillmore was their new showstopper. It wasn't only the acts on stage that excited theater-goers—they also knew that the first few rows were reserved for Tessie and Jessie's girls. On Sunday nights, which was the biggest theater night, Tessie and her rival would wait until the early acts started so they could make a grand entrance. Each madam would parade their beauties down separate aisles to take their seats.

The competitiveness between Tessie and Jessie grew over the next few years. Despite the Orpheum being relocated to downtown, it didn't stop the women from making their grand entrances. Like any good competitor, each tried to outwit the other. On one Sunday, Jessie arrived with her girls and strolled down their aisle and took their seats. The crowd waited with anticipation for Tessie to arrive, but she never did. The same thing happened the Sunday after that, and theater-goers had their curiosity piqued as to why Tessie and the girls were missing. Tessie had bested Jessie by skipping two Sundays and keeping her girls at home. Tessie played her game well, and on the third Sunday, it appeared Tessie would be a no-show again until midway through the show. Jessie and her girls were already seated when the show stopped, the lights went on, and the performers stopped. Jessie, her girls, and the entire theater turned around to see Tessie and her glamour girls waltz down the aisle. With their gowns rustling, feather boas flowing, and hats high on their heads, they made their grand entrance and literally stole the show. Despite Tessie winning the battle, their marketing plan worked, and both madams' houses were kept busy on Saturday and Sunday nights.[70]

As Tessie's wealth grew, so did her collection of expensive furniture and antiques. Her homes were bursting with lavishly decorated items she had collected. Some unique items included a green and white dinner service designed for William Rockefeller that bore his initials, as well as a large oil painting that King Leopold II of Belgium had given to the late Irish opera star Rose Cecelia Shay. She also enjoyed some famous local items, including draperies from the home of John D. Spreckels, who grew up in San Francisco, but later founded a transportation and real estate empire in San Diego (Spreckels's many business ventures included the Hotel del Coronado and the San Diego and Arizona Railway). She also had a bedroom set from one of San Francisco's most prominent philanthropists, William Henry Crocker. Her most bawdy item was a 600-pound buffet that was made of iron and was gilded in gold and decorated in amorous scenes. In order to satisfy her desire for acquiring luxury items, Tessie attended many auctions and art shops in the city. Her collectibles filled her homes to capacity, leaving scant room for her girls or patrons. In addition to her love of antiques, Tessie frequented her favorite department store as well. She was a regular at Gump's. A former buyer for Gump's named Ed Newell recalled Tessie, saying, "It wasn't that Tessie lacked taste. She had too much of it. She was under the impression that it could be compounded; if one thing was good ten just like it were ten times better. I don't recall any merchant foolish enough to tell her otherwise." Tessie didn't stop at filling her homes with expensive items. She also proudly wore a diamond tiara that once belonged to a European duchess and adorned herself with various diamond rings, necklaces, and bracelets. She also owned a topaz and pearl necklace and multiple furs.[71] Her love of diamonds was almost as indulgent as that of her rival Jessie Hayman's.

When "Big Frank" Daroux walked into Tessie's life, both of their lives would be changed forever—and not in the way they expected. They were a formidable pair. He was a well-known gambler and man about town and was big in both stature and size. She was one of San Francisco's top madams. In the early 1900s, Tessie and Frank began seeing each other. On their first date she recalled, "The night I first met Daroux he bought twenty-two bottles of wine. I bought some, too."[72] Some thirty years later, the story became exaggerated when the *San Francisco Chronicle* quoted Tessie as saying, "Frank bought me

120 bottles of champagne the night we first met."[73] Early during their courtship, Frank gave Tessie a glorious bed, which was a fantastic addition to her collection. It had once belonged to Napoleon, and its headpiece was gilded and decorated in swans and simpering cupids. That Napoleon bed and her adoration of Frank would be the start of Tessie's obsession with busts of the man from France. She soon began collecting busts of Napoleon because she claimed they reminded her of "Frankie." In the end, she would end up with more than two dozen.[74] She also had a custom brooch made that cost her $400. It was a miniature ivory image of Frank surrounded by diamonds.[75]

Although her first try at marriage ended in desertion and divorce in 1898, Tessie agreed to marry Frank. She wanted a grand wedding, but the family of the forty-eight-year-old groom said no. They would allow the marriage only as long as it was in another state and the newlyweds never mentioned it. Tessie reluctantly agreed because she was in love and wanted to be with Frank. They slipped away to Philadelphia, and on August 4, 1909, Tessie and Frank were married in a civil ceremony—far away from his family in northern California. The forty-year-old madam kept their marriage secret for a while after she said "I do," but Tessie still longed for a grand wedding.

A year later, the secretly married Tessie Wall was living and earning a nice income at her new brothel on 337 O'Farrell Street. She claimed to take in between $5,000 and $6,000 per month at her three-story brick and terra-cotta building.[76] The first floor was meant to be a saloon, but she didn't use it very often. The second floor was the main floor of the home, where Tessie's suite was located, as well as a kitchen, dining room, parlors, and a fully mirrored ballroom. What her customers wanted was on the third floor, which contained twelve bedrooms. Her girls were mostly described as "young, plump, and blonde."[77] Tessie, however, knew that diversity mattered, so she offered brunettes as well. She employed about fourteen girls, but that number varied. Some of the girls included Black Gladys, Elsie Woods, Mabel Ainsley, Grace Perry, Lila Agnews, Josephine Morton, Belle Adams, Lillie Emery, Viva Pruchott, Lucille Talbot, and Clara Thomas. Clara, like so many other girls, suffered from the "mental anguish" of her occupation. Despite her beautiful surroundings at 337 O'Farrell and her elegant trousseau, Clara was prone to jealousy and melancholia. At 6:30 on a spring morning, she swallowed a large quantity of mercury bichloride tablets to end her life. Tessie had her rushed to Central Emergency Hospital, where her stomach was pumped, and she later recovered.[78]

Tessie continued to long for a "proper" wedding, and two years after their Philadelphia nuptials, Frank finally consented to a church wedding. Tessie chose to wed on August 4, which was the anniversary of their civil ceremony. She wanted to be wed at a church and under the eyes of God and before the world, where they would become Mr. and Mrs. Frank Daroux.[79] But they had a hard time finding a Catholic church or a priest who would marry them. Finally, in 1912, St. Mary's Cathedral agreed, but the priest was worried about Tessie's reputation, so he set some conditions to their nuptials. First, he wouldn't hold the ceremony in the church itself, but he would marry them in the rectory and only witnesses could attend. Frank also set conditions on their marriage. He told Tessie she had to give up the madam business. She reluctantly agreed and sold her property in May.[80] When she learned that Frank had bought her a home in San Mateo she exclaimed, "San Mateo! Why, I'd sooner be under one electric light on Powell Street than own all of San Mateo!"

In exchange for all her concessions, Tessie made demands of Frank. She wanted her invited guests who could not attend the ceremony to be allowed to wait for them outside the church so they could wish them well. Tessie also wanted a band to play her favorite song, "Hail, Hail, the Gang's All Here," as she and Frank exited the church. Frank made many wedding day promises to Tessie and he broke them all. He did buy them a new home at 535 Powell Street where they would live and Tessie could enjoy her retirement. Their reception was held at a downtown restaurant, where 105 guests consumed about 960 bottles of champagne. Their cake weighed 150 pounds, and Frank's gift to Tessie was a $10,000 pearl necklace. The couple eventually slipped off to their Powell Street home only to find several wagonloads of manure dumped near the door by Frank's "Tenderloin" buddies. The couple left for a Canadian Rockies honeymoon, but because they fought so much, they returned home a month early.[81] Once back home, it appears that Tessie took up being a madam again until December 1915, when she was promised a cruise on Henry Ford's chartered ocean liner, the *Oscar II*, which the media nicknamed the "Peace Ship." This time Frank insisted that she sell her establishment in exchange for her cruise. She agreed, but then Frank declined Ford's invitation and Tessie was highly annoyed.

Despite her ups and downs with Frank, Tessie had one constant highlight in her life, and that was being the unofficial queen of the annual policeman's ball. Tessie with her tiara, diamonds, and champagne, along with the always smiling mayor, "Sunny Jim" Rolph, led the grand march. She enjoyed this honor until the day she died.

About four years after their church wedding, one of Tessie's loyal servants shared some information that devastated her. While their marriage was fraught with fights and turbulence, Tessie never suspected that her beloved Frank would have been stepping out with another woman. Tessie had her servant obtain the phone number of Frank's mistress, Mary Lind. Tessie being Tessie, she called Mary Lind and demanded that she come to their Powell Street home or she would find the woman and pay her a visit. Not wanting Tessie at her home, Mary agreed to come to Tessie's house. Once there, both she and Frank vehemently denied anything was going on between them. Tessie didn't believe them and told them that if she ever heard that this woman was "bothering" Frank, Tessie would kill her. Not long after, Frank moved into the St. Francis Hotel in early 1917 and, in the midst of the city's effort to clean up vice, filed for a divorce, citing cruelty on Tessie's part. Of course, Tessie had no intention of giving Frank a divorce, but her attorneys advised her to counter by asking for $400 per month for maintenance, $5,000 for attorney fees, and a return of $25,000 cash and many of her jewels. Tessie reluctantly agreed and also demanded the return of her $10,000 diamond necklace, a $3,200 diamond sunburst, a $2,200 diamond square ring, two $1,500 rough cut diamonds, a $400 diamond handbag, and two diamond bracelets valued at $800. Their real estate holdings in San Francisco, as well as Sacramento, Kentfield, and Suisun City, were also part of the negotiation.

Tessie continued to live at the couple's Powell Street home with a friend named I. J. Simmons. Since Tessie and Frank were both well-known local characters, their divorce proceedings were talked about around town, in the courts, and in the papers. By February, Tessie couldn't bear the thought of living without Frank, so she tried to reconcile with him. When he turned her down during an unsuccessful phone call, Tessie did the only thing a desperate woman would do; she grabbed a carving knife and began slicing her wrists. Simmons caught Tessie in the midst of trying to commit suicide and wrangled the knife from her. He got her settled and called the doctor, who bandaged her wrists and put the very hysterical Tessie to bed.[82]

Tessie recovered from her physical wounds but would gain new emotional ones as the divorce court proceedings began. Things became uncomfortable for Tessie when, in May, her sister Mary Donohue-O'Connor testified that Tessie was verbally abusive to Frank, often threw her diamonds at him, and was frequently intoxicated. Her sister-in-law, Margaret Donohue, also originally testified that Tessie drank too much, but also noted that Tessie was sober during the six weeks that Frank had been ill and hospitalized.[83] Tessie claimed that she "took the pledge" in April 1916 and had only one drink per day.[84] Tessie's pledge of one drink per day is a tad bit different from most people's version of the pledge, but then Tessie was different from people in many ways. She was quoted as saying, "I never saw the day when I couldn't walk, and you are never drunk until somebody has to assist you along."[85]

After long court days and negotiations, both Frank and Tessie's attorneys tried to settle the divorce, but Tessie refused because she would not admit she was cruel. She really didn't think she was. Frank said he married Tessie only because she threatened to jump out of a window of the Knickerbocker Hotel in New York City unless he agreed. Tessie endured the hurtful words from her family and from Frank, and in one testimony he called her a German submarine after her outburst at a Market Street billiard parlor. The papers reported that Tessie had arrived late to view a parade from the upper story of the billiard parlor, but, unable to find a good seat, she had exploded and created a scene worthy of a submarine attack.[86] Finally, and much to Tessie's shock and dislike, the judge ruled in Frank's favor and granted him a divorce due to Tessie's extreme cruelty, on June

16, 1917. Frank was legally a free man, but this wasn't the end for Tessie—she refused to acknowledge the divorce and continued to try to win Frank back.

That same year, shortly after Thanksgiving, Tessie went to see Mary Lind at her home. Tessie claimed she had fallen on hard times over the divorce and only had $1.60 to her name. She was determined to make sure that her ex-husband's mistress Mary knew all about her devastating life. After all, Mary had been secretly seeing her husband for three or four years and Tessie was desperate. As she waited for Mary to arrive home, she was saddened and infuriated when she saw Frank and Mary step off the streetcar together. An infuriated Tessie ran up to them and shouted, "Now at last I've caught you!"

Frank, not wanting to face Tessie, immediately ran up the stairs to Mary's house and went inside. Mary did not retreat, but rather she stood her ground and faced an angry Tessie. Battle lines were drawn between the two women who loved Frank. Mary was the aggressor and she threatened to horsewhip Tessie if she ever showed up at her house again. Tessie didn't back down and responded with, "You've got my husband, and you'll get it back some day. It's not right." The hostility didn't end there, and the next day, Tessie received a threatening call from Mary. After that, it appeared it was over.[87]

As the Christmas season was upon San Francisco, Tessie went shopping, but not for clothes, toys, or antiques. Instead, she purchased a revolver from a store on Third Street in mid-December. A few days later, she decided she needed to see Frank in person and took her new purchase just in case she ran into the angry Mary Lind. Tessie waited for him across the street from his hotel, and as he walked down Powell Street, she followed him, pleading and begging for Frank to give her their house at Geary and Jones so she could make an honest living. He told her no and that she could beg on the streets before he would give her a dime. No doubt his words stung Tessie as he threatened to "put her far away from everyone" if she appealed the divorce. He had had enough of Tessie and walked away. As he strolled down Anna Lane near the Tivoli Theater, a shot rang out and Frank never knew what hit him. Tessie fired her new revolver into Frank's back. Tessie's hurt and anger had been percolating for some time, which caused her to shoot the man she loved and adored. One shot wasn't enough to quell the hurt, and when Frank turned around to hold himself up, Tessie leveled her gun and put two more rounds into his chest. Tessie stood there, and when the police arrived, she said, "Sure, I shot him. Why? Because I love him—damn him, how I love him!"[88]

During his recovery, she tried to visit Frank, but he would not allow her anywhere near him. She was crushed at the news. He slowly recovered, and despite the fact that she admitted to shooting him and was booked for attempted murder, Frank wanted to sever all ties to Tessie. He refused to press charges and married Mary Lind. Frank moved to New York City for a while, but later returned to Sacramento where his family lived.

Tessie was free to move on with her life in San Francisco, but she never forgot Frank. As a reminder, she kept a large portrait of him over her fireplace and many of the Napoleon busts around her house. Tessie moved into 442 London Street and stayed there for at least two years. In an unusual twist, Tessie lived with Joseph J. Wall, who was likely the brother of her first husband Edward, along with his wife Mary and their son John. In 1922, Tessie moved into a small apartment at 3569 18th Street, one of her properties in the old Mission District, where she grew up. Tessie continued to entertain and even operated a speakeasy during Prohibition, serving Canadian whiskey to close friends. She lived there for nearly ten years.

Tessie's life continued to be filled with drama. An unusual situation arose in 1922 when Maria McCarthy passed away. Tessie was the godmother of Maria's son, Joseph Lawrence McCarthy. Upon Maria's death, however, Joseph came forward and claimed that he was actually Tessie's son. Joseph claimed that Maria McCarthy was only his foster mother and that when she died, he had learned the truth. What we know today is that the 1900 census shows a Joseph L. McCarthy living with his parents Jeremiah and Maria. Oddly, Joseph L. McCarthy enlisted in the U.S. Army in 1918 as Joseph Lawrence Wall, yet later claimed that it wasn't until Maria's death in 1922 that he learned his true identity. He was living in New York City when he enlisted during WWI at Fort Slocum on January 6, 1918. No war records could be found for Joseph L. McCarthy.[89] Tessie denied that she was his mother and sought a suit to stop him from making any claim on her or her estate. It's curious that census records show that Joseph McCarthy was born in July 1887—a year after Tessie's own son was born and died.

To his dying day, Joseph Lawrence McCarthy insisted that Tessie was his mother. Even his death certificate listed his name as Joseph Lawrence Wall. The death certificate also listed Tessie's son's birthdate and listed Edward M. and Teresa S. Donohue-Wall as his parents. This man, claiming to be Tessie's son, died just five days shy of his ninetieth birthday. During his lifetime, he served in WWI, married Sylvia M. Foster (who died in 1959), and worked as a teamster. At the time of his death, he had been living on Guerrero Street in San Francisco.[90]

Was Tessie's son still alive or did her godson, Joseph McCarthy, take her son's name in the 1900s and claim it until his death? Or was it all a scheme by Maria McCarthy to ensure her son would inherit some of his godmother's money by posing as her son? This part of history remains a true mystery. Tessie vehemently denied that this man was her son and claimed she was only his godmother. She even stated in her last will and testament that anyone who successfully laid claim as her child only be given $1 from her estate.

Tessie's beloved Frank traveled to Paris, France, in 1928 and, like many passengers, connected through New York City on his way back home to California. He arrived in New York in October, but he never made it home, dying in New York.[91] Despite being divorced, Tessie had continued calling herself Mrs. Frank Daroux, and when he died, she went from calling herself his wife to his widow, truly showing that she clung to her love for him her entire life.

Four years after Frank passed, Tessie died on April 28, 1932, at her home on 3569 18th Street after having some dental work done. Some sources cited the dental work as the cause of her death, but the official records show she died of chronic myocarditis, which could have been caused from a bacterial infection. Other listed causes of death included blockages in her heart, a blockage in her kidney, and chronic pancreatitis, which can be caused by excessive alcohol use.

Gilded to the end, Tessie was laid to rest in a gold casket in

Tessie Donohue's granite and marble grave marker at Greenlawn Memorial Park.
PHOTOGRAPH BY SHERRY MONAHAN.

Greenlawn Memorial Park in Colma, in section Palm III. Her last will and testament stipulated that she be buried alongside her infant son. Curiously, there is no Joseph Lawrence Wall buried by her, but there is an L. Wall, who was moved from the Odd Fellows Cemetery, which stopped interments in 1910. The cemetery records are vague and no other details exist about the identity of L. Wall. Her brother William J., sister Sarah, and mother Sarah, along with someone named Foley, are also buried with her.[92]

ANNIE MAY WYANT, AKA DIAMOND JESSIE

Beautiful, gray-eyed Annie May Wyant was born in Louisiana. Beyond that, much of what we know about Diamond Jessie's life is confusing or downright conflicting. Her funeral records show she was born around 1867 in New Orleans, yet her passport application indicates she was born 140 miles to the west on December 9, 1874, in Lafayette Parish. Many accounts claim she was a redhead, yet her passport states her hair was brown. It's possible she was a redhead early on and then later she dyed it brown. What *is* known about Annie is that she stood five feet, five inches tall and had an oval face and chin. She also used many names during her lifetime—including Jessie Mellon and Jessie Hayman—and at some point, made her legal name Annie May Mellon.

Annie began her working girl career as a prostitute named Jessie Mellon in Nina Hayman's establishment at 225 Ellis Street in San Francisco. She earned the respect of Nina as a working girl, but also as a woman with business savvy. By 1898, Nina retired and Jessie took her boss's last name and ran the house. Jessie Mellon was now Jessie Hayman. Her girls included the twenty-year-old P. Neumann from California, twenty-one-year-old M. Lenard from Oregon, and twenty-two-year-old M. Rosenstock from Nebraska. An F. Livingston, who was a twenty-seven-year-old, and F. Silva, twenty-five, both from Mexico, completed Jessie's entourage at this time.

It's not known exactly when, but early on Jessie became enamored with a wealthy socialite engineer named Allan St. John Bowie, and he with her. Allan lived at his new home at the corner of Gough Street and Pacific Avenue, but he stayed there for only a couple of years, and then later he moved to 1909 Jackson Street. If you believe Jessie's passport details, she claims they were married in 1899. While no iron-clad proof of their union exists, there is plenty to connect the two. The *Chronicle* reported that Mr. St. John Bowie took up rooms next door to Jessie's Ellis Street place when she took it over from Nina Hayman. The rooms were far below St. John Bowie's station, in an old wooden building at the corner of Taylor Street. He spent time at both of his residences.[93]

In 1900, Allan's sister, Helen "Jessie," divorced her husband, and she and her two children, Charles Bowie Detrick and Mary Helen Detrick, moved in with Allan. They all lived at the Jackson Street home for many years, and Allan's brother Augustus also lived with him for a time. As a bachelor and man of some means, Allan employed two servants to look after the household. He also made frequent trips to Asia, in part to visit his father and another brother who lived in Japan. He traveled there in the summer of 1902 and returned in August.[94]

Allan and Jessie continued their relationship and on June 2, 1903, Annie May "Jessie" Mellon purchased the lot at 2300 Post Street at the corner of Divisadero from Allan St. John Bowie for a mere $10.[95] Because it was a corner lot, she had doors on both sides and her address was also given as 1601 Divisadero Street. Once she settled in to her new house and got her business going, she and Allan took a trip together to Japan. On their way back home, they had their trunks loaded on the train and boarded the *Chicago Limited*, which traveled at an astonishing speed of fifty miles per hour toward St. Louis. As passengers were sitting down for supper at 7 P.M. on July 4, 1904, their train hit a switch and collided with a freight train. Flames engulfed many of the cars. The wreck left several people dead and many more were injured. Both Jessie and Allan escaped unharmed, but they did lose all their luggage in the fire. When the flames were extinguished and passengers cared for, the remaining travelers were rebooked. Jessie and Allan were able to continue home and later filed claims against the railroad for damages to their luggage.[96] Once Jessie was back in San Francisco, she settled back into her madamship.

It was around this time that a massive scandal shook San Francisco. It became public knowledge that the city tax collector, Edward H.

Smith, had been embezzling thousands of dollars. Smith had also become enamored with a prostitute named Leona Brooks, who had once worked for Jessie at her Ellis Street brothel. Smith, with his new-found money, had set up his "countess" in proper style at an apartment on Jones and Pine Streets, and she began calling herself Mrs. Gunther. Her primary visitor was none other than Jessie Hayman, and during December 1904 and January 1905, the pair were often seen on the streets together, sporting their finest clothing and jewels.

But then on March 5, 1905, Jessie sold her 225 Ellis Street brothel. She and Allan traveled back to St. Louis to contest their still outstanding luggage claims. The pair checked into the Planter's Hotel in St. Louis and registered as Mr. and Mrs. J. Bowie.[97]

Two months later, Edward Smith was feeling an imminent threat to his future and freedom, so he and Leona Brooks left San Francisco and fled to St. Louis around the same time Jessie and Allan were there. When Jessie learned what was happening, she went to Brooks's rescue and was interviewed by the Pinkertons, who were handling the Smith case. The detectives contacted Jessie only because she was a friend of Brooks. The Pinkertons assured a *Chronicle* reporter that even though Jessie Hayman was connected to the Smith case, using the name of Lena Bowie, she was not suspected of receiving any of the money.

Because Bowie's name had been brought up, speculation about Jessie and Allan's relationship began to swirl. On May 13, 1905, a supposed friend and anonymous club buddy of Allan's submitted an editorial to the *Oakland Tribune*. He flat-out stated that both Jessie Hayman and Allan were his good friends and, in fact, Jessie had become Mrs. Allan St. John Bowie, although he didn't recall when, but was sure it was after 1902. He wrote, "I don't think there is a better-hearted woman than Mrs. Bowie." He claimed that Bowie first met Jessie about six or seven years ago and could talk of nothing or no one else. His friends and family knew who Jessie was and did not want Allan to marry her. They paraded plenty of heiresses around him, made him attend parties to meet the proper women, and more. It did no good—he had fallen for the sensual Jessie. His friend claimed that around 1902 Bowie and Jessie, along with her chaperone, traveled to

China and Japan, where Bowie had relatives. His friend concluded with, "If I have gained one convert to my viewpoint as a result of this, my first literary effort, I am well repaid for my labor. I feel in my heart of hearts that this epistle has done my friend, Allan St. John Bowie, good." The anonymous scribe refused to give his name for fear of being attacked in the papers like his friend Allan had been.[98]

An opposing opinion appeared in the *Oakland Tribune* several days later claiming that Allan was *not* married to Jessie, but was *involved* with her. They claimed that Bowie insisted he was not married to Jessie and had successfully convinced his friends of that. The reporter claimed that Allan was sorry he registered as Mr. and Mrs. Bowie and should have used an alias. The couple were working with a Pinkerton detective in St. Louis on their luggage claims when Jessie's old friend Leona Brooks arrived. Safely back in San Francisco, Allan and his sister Helen "Jessie" set sail for a European trip—quite possibly to leave the scandal behind.[99]

While Allan sailed to Europe, Jessie remained in San Francisco and, while at her Post Street location, was brought before the courts on multiple charges during District Attorney Langdon's war on the "dens of vice." His initial push was to arrest only the madams to get to the root of the problem. On September 5, 1906, Jessie was made an example and became the first madam, without her girls, to be arrested, but she paid her fine and kept entertaining clients. Two months later, a man named Henry Goldman brought an injunction against Mrs. A. M. Mellon and Allan St. John Bowie, who he claimed were the joint property owners of her brothel. He stated that he had signed a seven-year lease for the first floor and the side yard from them on March 1, 1906, to operate a saloon. After the big earthquake on April 18, however, Jessie began erecting additional rooms and knocking down a portion of the wall and the entrance to his business, which was practically blocked.[100]

While the case was being decided, Jessie dealt with being arrested yet again in January 1907, along with her girls this time, who included Mary Reed, Ethel Evans, and Helen Clark.[101] Once again, Allan's name was brought into the fray. They were named as codefendants and both testified during the trial in Judge James Troutt's court. Bowie admitted that he had acted as Jessie's agent in drawing up the lease. Documentary evidence also confirmed that saloonkeeper Goldman and Bowie were the ones who conducted all the business concerning the lease.[102] The ordeal continued, despite the judge finding in favor of Goldman, when Jessie had two workers tear down a fence and begin brickwork. When Goldman complained to the judge, Troutt directed Sheriff O'Neil to investigate. Feeling the pressure to move, Jessie relocated and purchased the Glenwood Hotel at 44 Mason Street.[103] As most madams did, Jessie often hired new girls, and she made a new addition to her staff when she brought "musician" Ethel May Southwood. She claimed that Ethel was hired to sing and play the piano for her clients. When Ethel arrived in March, she went straight to work for Jessie.

The moral crusade continued and Jessie remained a target. In August 1908, she experienced multiple incidents at her Glenwood Hotel. One of her girls, Georgia Spencer, tried to kill herself with an overdose of morphine. Jessie called for help and had Georgia rushed to the hospital where they pumped her stomach and gave her permanganate of potash. The hospital staff was surprised to hear a known prostitute cry out for a husband, since they knew she was from Jessie's house. They ignored her at first, thinking she was delirious, but Georgia insisted they contact Robert Sheldon, who was a well-to-do real estate agent. They did, and Robert came and moved her to a private hospital.[104]

Jessie's brothel was quiet for only about a week when she was arrested for harboring an alien prostitute in a disreputable house. That "alien" was none other than her new musician, Ethel May Southwood. Shortly after midnight on August 26, federal officers raided Jessie's brothel on Mason and arrested her for harboring Ethel, who was from England. The federal statute prohibited anyone from harboring and maintaining a house of ill fame and housing an alien who hadn't been in the country for at least three years. It was a serious offense when enforced and carried a heavy fine of $5,000, along with possible imprisonment. Jessie, of course, claimed she did not know that Ethel May was an alien. Allan St. John Bowie came to Jessie's rescue and put up a $10,000 bond. It's possible Allan was simply repaying a debt to Jessie because she had lent him $12,000 back in February when he wanted to expand the south side of Jackson where his house stood. It was a true loan and the terms were for one year at five percent interest.[105]

Jessie wasn't the only madam affected, and several other madams with foreign inmates were also arrested during the crusade.[106] During Jessie's ordeal, investigators learned that Ethel May Southwood had been working at a brothel in Chicago prior to arriving in San Francisco, but she still had not been in the States long enough. Jessie was indicted and charged with her crime in September. While the case was being argued, Southwood, whose alias was Bonnie Pelham, was ordered to be deported but not until the case was closed. By mid-December, Jessie was found guilty of harboring an alien and Ethel was promptly deported. Jessie was also ordered to pay a $300 fine and spend thirty days in jail, which was minimal considering the offense's much stiffer maximum fine and jail time.

It's curious that in 1910 Jessie does not appear to have been living at her Glenwood Hotel, yet there are several women under the age of thirty living there. It's possible that she traveled to the Orient again or to another destination. Regardless of where Jessie was, the eldest "manicurist" at her home was thirty-year-old Dorothy Rothschild from Kentucky. Also living there was Maxine Fairchild, twenty-three, from Minnesota; Ruth Coleman, who claimed to be a singer, twenty-seven and a Kentucky native; Maggie M. Nevine, a twenty-four-year-old milliner from Florida; and Genevieve Dare, nineteen, who claimed to be from Missouri.

The following year Jessie moved to a three-story brick building at 130 Eddy where she stayed for six years. This was one of Jessie's most exotic brothels and was where Lee Francis, the well-known Hollywood madam, got her start and lifelong lessons. It sported a wine cellar filled with French champagne and wine from all over the world. Customers passed through the doors of her house and into the first-floor saloon. Stairs led them to the brothel occupying the next two floors. Jessie's décor in this house was ornately designed, and rooms were named for their themes. Patrons could spend time in a red room, blue room, Oriental room, Turkish room, or gold room.

Lee once said it was "a real Place Pigalle," which was, and still is, Paris's red-light district. Jessie's own red and gold Pompeiian room, as well as the plush parlors, were on the second floor and welcomed clients to an exotic experience with Oriental couches, shaded lamps, and deep carpets on the floor. The dining room and bedrooms on the third floor also reflected the tone of the house so clients could still feel the effects of Place Pigalle. Each girl rented a suite from Jessie for $5 per day. Jessie set the fee that was charged to her clients and the girls kept the remainder of what they earned. She also made her money by charging clients for food and wine while they were in her house. The girls' routine was regular and began with them dressing and appearing in their full regal attire. When ready, they descended to the second-floor parlors where they would sit and wait for the clients to show up, starting around 9 P.M. While most of Jessie's girls were chosen by the clients, she had a few $15 girls who could choose their own clients. When the house closed at 4 A.M., the girls were done working. To clean up and get refreshed, they soaked in lavender salts and were massaged by their maids. They tucked into bed, went to sleep, and their routine started all over again the next day.[107]

With her business running smoothly, Jessie traveled to the Orient once again. On her return to the States, she departed from Hong Kong as Mrs. Anna May Mellon on July 5, 1914. The thirty-eight-year-old madam boarded the SS *Manchuria* with sixteen pieces of luggage. Her claimed age would indicate she was born in 1876.[108] Jessie returned home and continued to earn a good deal of money and buy diamonds until about 1917, when she retired and moved to a large apartment building at 1096 Pine. She lived there as Mrs. Anna M. Mellon, and in 1921, for reasons unknown, she listed herself as Jessie M. Bowie, widow of John.

A year later, in late October 1922, Jessie waltzed into the U.S. Department of State office in San Francisco to apply for a passport. She wore a dark hat topped with small peacock feathers. She and a friend of two years named Jacob Shaen swore that Jessie was the wife of Allan St. John Bowie and that they had been married in 1899. She also claimed this was the first time she had applied for a passport, although she had traveled to Asia in 1914 with Allan; in this era, wives

The only known image of Annie May Wyant, aka Diamond Jessie, from her passport application. PHOTOGRAPH COURTESY OF THE NATIONAL ARCHIVES AND RECORDS ADMINISTRATION.

were sometimes listed on their husbands' passports. Also, in general, the United States did not require passports for foreign travel until World War I (1914–1918), and then that requirement lapsed in 1921. Many other countries did require a passport for entry, and Jessie was preparing for a globetrotting trip to visit Japan, China, Hong Kong, India, France, Denmark, and finally Sweden. Her two beloved cats, Beppo and Teddy, would be her traveling companions.

After her tour, Jessie stayed at the Hotel Cecil in London. Every night while she was there, Jessie donned her finest dresses, sported her many diamonds, and ate in the dining room. The night of March 31, 1923, ended differently. Jessie dressed for dinner in a beautiful gown and all her diamonds—just like she had the previous evenings. She sat in her chair in her hotel room, apparently waiting for the proper time to go down to the dining room. But she never appeared in the dining room, and a maid found her still sitting in her chair dressed for dinner. She had died of heart failure. Her cats were reportedly devastated but were well cared for by a relative back in the States.

Jessie, like her competitor Tessie Wall, had amassed a fortune in expensive collectibles. An auction after her death included a Louis XV French rosewood table, a carved Louis XVI Italian walnut table, Italian walnut living room chairs, Sevres porcelain vases chiseled with bronze mountings, French commodes with marble tops, a frieze mohair living room suite, a pair of Louis XV walnut flower stands, a Chickering piano, a Mulberry velour living room suite, mirrors, Wilton rugs, Chinese rugs, a grandfather clock, a complete set of white and gold Limoges china, Lenox and Sheffield tea sets, Shreve silver, a Kreiss dawn gray bed suite, a rose silk boudoir chair, hair mattresses, fancy gowns, a chinchilla wrap, and a multitude of other foreign antiques.[109]

Jessie left $15,000 in a trust from her estate to her niece Linda Wyant, who was a minor. Linda's father (Jessie's brother) was a janitor named Charles Wyant. The remainder of her $200,000 estate was divided among other relatives. She also left $1,000 for the care of her beloved cats. She was buried alone in Cypress Lawn Memorial Park in Colma. Even after her death, there was still doubt as to whether Jessie and Allan were ever married. In April 1923, safely after her death, the *Santa Cruz News* reported, "Allan St. John Bowie, prominent club man, to whom Miss Hayman is said to have been engaged, denied today she was his wife."[110]

Three years after Jessie died, Bowie married Anita Imelda Hughes, a woman half his age, on May 29, 1926. They resided in a $50,000 home on Black Mountain Road in Hillsborough, where he employed a maid, a cook, and a gardener. The couple had a son in 1927, but their marriage grew rocky and in 1935, she sued for divorce. The pair eventually reconciled, but perhaps only so that Anita could hold on to Allan's fortune. Allan died on February 10, 1938, in Hillsborough, and was buried in Holy Cross Cemetery in Colma, then later interred in St. Mary's Cemetery in Oakland. After Allan's death, his sister Helen "Jessie" claimed that both Anita and her mother were frauds.

2

Sacramento

Sacramento's population boomed when gold was found at Sutter's Mill in 1848. A gold rush pioneer recalled his 1849 arrival: "At the time of our arrival, on the 15th of August, at the 'Embarcadero,' as Sacramento was then called, there was not a frame building in the town, except a small one-story structure, where Sam Brannan kept a store. . . . There was a rush from the mines, coming after stores, or to have a grand carouse. All had gold dust, and nearly all drank whisky. It was no uncommon occurrence to see a miner call up every person around and spend an ounce or two in treating."[111] By 1854, the mining camp had become the state capital, and in 1863 the Central Pacific Railroad broke ground at Front and K Streets.

Sacramento was a railroad, riverboat, and capital city that became a business hub where men traded and businesses enjoyed explosive growth. Of course, single miners, freighters, and sailors all became lonely, and there were women who were ready to play their wife or mistress—for a fee. While most men in town were happy to see the madams and their demimonde arrive, some were not so keen on it. As the town grew, churches, civic organizations, and more turned this wharf town into a sophisticated city.

The police were being pressured to get the brothels in town under control, so they stationed officers outside of them. In the summer of 1870, Sacramento's madams and owners of the brothels worked out an agreement with Chief of Police Crowley to calm the tension between the two opposing forces. The madams promised to keep their doors closed, curtains down, and their employees invisible to people on the street, so long as the officers who had been stationed outside their establishments were withdrawn and their surveillance ended.[112] Two years later, in 1872, the Sacramento Board of Police Commissioners met and created and amended the rules by which their officers would conduct themselves in and around town. The rules included uniform protocols, taking time off, arrest procedures, and other typical rules. Section 13 addressed where they couldn't go while they were in uniform, except during the course of doing their job. The new rule prevented them from entering saloons, theaters, drinking houses, houses of ill fame, balls, circuses, or any other place of entertainment.[113]

One particular madam in town faced the law on multiple occasions; her name was Eugenie Dubois. She was causing problems as early as 1872, when she was arrested for violating an unspecified city ordinance. Her next recorded brush with the law came in the summer of 1873, when she was arrested for disturbing the peace and also for keeping a house of ill fame. She pleaded guilty to disturbing the peace, but her ill fame case was held over and she posted a $100 bond.[114]

Because of women like Eugenie, the city had begun to crack down on vice by 1874, and it was happily reported that they arrested 2,527 people that year, up 173 more arrests than in 1872. Of those arrested, 500 were charged with disturbing the peace, 419 for being drunk, 15 for exposure, and 30 for enticing people into houses of ill fame. One person was arrested for keeping a house of ill fame and eight for living in one.[115] Despite the progress being made with arrests, the law didn't move fast enough for some residents and they took matters into their own hands. As the night of May 24, 1874, was winding down, someone touched a match to the front parlor curtains in Mary

Schwartz's brothel on the south side of L Street, between Second and Third Streets. Around 10 P.M. the fire alarm was sounded, and the fire was quickly put out without the use of the fire engines. Minimal damage was done, and Mary needed only to replace two sets of curtains, paint the scorched window frames, and remove the soot from her plastered walls.

It was into this growing capital city that the following madams plied their trade.

LUCIE OCTAVE

Around 1866, a forty-something French immigrant named Lucie set up business in Sacramento. She began with a modest start. Today, Lucie's story exists only through mentions in newspapers about her finances or her brothel business.

Lucie wasn't destitute—her personal property was valued at $150 (about $2,300 in today's money). She paid her taxes just like everyone else, but the city gave her and other residents a shock when they created additional assessments for 1867. The city added $500 to Lucie's personal property value so her total jumped to $650.[116]

By 1869, the single madam was residing at 57 L Street, between Second and Third Streets. In the fall, she was arrested for disturbing the peace and paid a $20 fine.[117] The following year, the U.S. Census noted that Lucie was a woman of easy virtue, living with a thirty-five-year-old French woman of easy virtue named Mary Antoinette. Lucie did well that year and accumulated a tidy sum of $300.[118] By 1871 she relocated to 47 L Street, where she listed herself as a widow.[119] Three years later, she did what many madams did—got arrested. It was a hot August day in 1873 when Lucie was charged with disturbing the peace and keeping a house of ill fame. She was found not guilty on the disturbing the peace charge, and her ill fame case was held over and she posted a $100 bond.[120]

Lucie went to San Francisco in late 1880 and ended up in the French Hospital. It is unknown whether she traveled there because she was sick or began suffering symptoms after she arrived in the city. What is known is that Lucie died in the hospital of apoplexy or internal bleeding on December 7, 1880. This sixty-seven-year-old died intestate with an estate that included $900 in cash and $50 worth of household furnishings. A week after her death, a man named Jack Hammond was arrested on suspicion of having taken articles and funds from the estate of Madam Lucie.

Upon Lucie's death, W. B. Miller was named as the administrator in charge, but he let the case linger. When he died in 1897, the probate stalled. It wasn't until 1898 that another administrator was assigned to her estate. By that time, the estate only had $454.70, which went to the state because she had no will or heirs who came forward.[121, 122]

LIZZIE ROBERTS-GORDON, AKA LIZZIE THE LIVELY FLEA

Elizabeth "Lizzie" Roberts was born about 1841 in the state of New York. Lizzie arrived in Sacramento by 1869 after being run out of San Francisco, where she ran a disturbing, admission-based show with a woman named Kate Jolly (sometimes spelled Jollie). When she arrived in Sacramento, she hooked up with a sporting man named William Gordon and went by Lizzie Gordon when it suited her.

Her October 1868 arrest, along with her partner, Kate Jolly, both sickened and shocked many in San Francisco and in other parts of the state. Both were charged with indecent exposure, and her future home paper, the *Sacramento Daily Union* wrote, "The testimony is beyond revolting."[123] The *San Francisco Chronicle* was also disgusted, but went into a little more detail, and those details remain appalling even to this day. Their headline was, "Horrible Depravity. –Arrest of the Wickedest Women in the World." Lizzie and Kate performed an act that the reporter claimed was popular in France, called the Industrious Flea. The women charged a $5 admission to their Pine Street brothel, but they quickly relocated once they realized that police had learned the details of their deplorable business. They then moved their act to a house on Dupont Street, where a large room allowed paying spectators watch them do unspeakable things with an animal. The *Chronicle* wrote, "The particulars of the offense are so utterly filthy and bestial, that no decent language can be used to convey any idea of its utter depravity. . . . A large dog belonging to these vile wretches was not arrested."[124]

By 1869, Lizzie had landed in Sacramento. In December, she was arrested by Officer Burwick after she threw a tumbler into the large mirror at the back bar of the Empire Saloon on K Street near Second. It took Lizzie three months to exact revenge on Burwick, but she did. She and her paramour, Gordon, wandered into the Empire around midnight in February of 1870 and saw Burwick. Lizzie began hurling verbal assaults at him, along with bottles and tumblers. Lizzie and Gordon finally took down Burwick and began to pummel the officer until another officer, visiting from San Francisco, assisted. The two policemen then arrested Lizzie and Gordon.[125] After her arrest, and while she was released to await her trial, Lizzie was arrested by Officer Hickey for disturbing the peace, along with a woman named Cassie Doe. She and Gordon were tried in August, and many of the townspeople showed up to see what the lively hussy would do. Lizzie was convicted of vagrancy, but the jury could not agree one hundred percent on Gordon's complicity, so he was set free.[126] Lizzie was sentenced to twenty days in jail, but her attorney argued that there was only a jury of six, which was six shy of the twelve required by law. The court agreed and she was released.

Lizzie went back to running her brothel on Second Street between I and J Streets. In early 1871, she denied entry to a group of drunken men. They didn't take too kindly at being denied, so one of the men fired a pistol into her brothel. No one was injured, and no arrests were made in the incident. She was still in Sacramento in August that year—according to the newspaper, a Western Union telegram was waiting for Lizzie Roberts or Gordon. It's not known what happened to Lizzie. A death notice for a "Lizzie Gordon" appeared in Sacramento newspapers in 1875, but details in her will could not confirm whether this was the same woman.[127, 128]

CORA CONWAY-LEE

Cora Conway-Lee, who shares the name of a San Francisco madam of the same time, found herself in Sacramento in mid-1873. Despite the similar name and era, it's not likely these are the same woman, since the Cora Lee of San Francisco was of African descent and the Sacramento Cora was of Irish descent. It's not certain if Cora was a madam with girls or a sole prostitute, but her story shows just how dangerous and sad this lifestyle was.

Cora's hot temper frequently found her in and out of the court-room. In early May, she and a woman named Ida Scott were brought before a Sacramento judge and found guilty of disturbing the peace. The women had quarreled on Second Street, where they lived in ad-joining houses. As Cora walked past Ida and a man named Charles Roach, Ida allegedly called Cora a "Hibernian canine of the feminine gender" and threw some glasses at her. Roach afterwards hit Cora when she talked about the incident. Ida claimed that Cora disturbed her peace by throwing things at her. While Cora was arrested for dis-turbing the peace, Charles Roach was arrested for battery on Cora.[129,] [130] Just two months later, in July, Cora and Annie Stevens were ar-rested for violating an unspecified city ordinance.

Cora's time in Sacramento appeared to be over, so she moved to the town of Red Bluff, about midway between Sacramento and the Oregon border, where she briefly stayed. Apparently Red Bluff did not suit Cora, so she left toward the end of summer 1873 and made her way to Tehama. When she arrived there, she settled in at a sa-loon owned by Indiana native Dan Buckley. Like many prostitutes and madams, Cora caught the man's eye and Dan soon fell in love with her. Thirty-seven-year-old Dan stood five feet, four inches tall, but he carried a tall temper. Cora soon moved out and set up her brothel, but Dan didn't like her taking on clients and threatened to shoot her, which he attempted a few times without success. Buckley may have been short in stature, but he was long on perseverance and, unfortu-nately for Cora, he finally succeeded on October 21, 1873. The *Red Bluff Independent* reported, "The particulars of the case and causes which led to the shooting are such as to hardly make it proper for us to publish." Prior to killing Cora, Buckley had been on a drinking binge for at least a week and quarreled with her almost daily. It was a cool Tuesday afternoon when he loaded a shotgun and called on Cora. When she opened the door, Buckley pointed the gun at her but did not fire. She told him to go away, and if he came back again, she would have him arrested.

Deputy Sheriff Clark heard what was going on and advised Cora to have Buckley arrested, but she refused because she intended to leave town in two days and didn't want any trouble. Just before 4 P.M. that same day, Deputy Clark was on his way home and saw Buckley come from the rear of his saloon with a shotgun. He asked Buckley where he was going, to which Buckley replied he was going to shoot some quail for his supper. Clark wasn't convinced, so he watched as Buckley passed by Cora's place and went some distance beyond the house. Assuming Buckley was truly out hunting for his dinner, Clark proceeded home. After reaching his house, Clark noticed Buckley returning, and, anticipating trouble, started toward Cora's. When Cora's house came into sight, Clark noticed the door open and saw Cora standing in it. Buckley, by this time had come to within a few feet of the house. Clark couldn't see Buckley because he was shielded by a pile of lumber, but he did hear the gunshot and saw Cora stagger into a room. As he ran toward the house, he saw Buckley running to his saloon with his gun in his hands. Clark saw that Cora was shot and ran off to arrest Buckley. Details of what happened were provided by an unnamed man who was in the house with Cora. He claimed that when Buckley came near the door, Cora opened it and had a few words with Buckley, who then raised his gun and fired point blank at Cora. When she saw the gun, she turned partly around, probably with the intention of placing the door between them, but he was too quick for her. As the shot struck her, she said, "I am dead," and the unnamed man caught her in his arms and laid her on the floor. He rushed out of the house to get Dr. Cottle, who arrived and pronounced her wound fatal. She was shot in the left arm and breast, with pellets penetrating her heart and lungs. The paper reported, "The gun must have been heavily loaded as the flesh on the arm is all shot to pieces and nearly fifty shot wounds appears in the breast, while the wall in the rear of the door shows the marks of as many more. Efforts were made immediately after the shooting to get a statement from the woman, but internal hemorrhaging prevented her speaking more than a few words. She stated that Buckley shot her, and then requested that word of her death be sent to her father."[131]

During his trial, Buckley did not deny shooting Cora, but he claimed that she shot at him with the revolver that was found at her side when she fell to the floor. However, witnesses stated they heard only one shot. When the *Red Bluff Sentinel* reporter visited Buckley in jail, he pleaded his case. Buckley stated that he and Cora fought all the time, and the evening before her death, she had chased him with a knife. Immediately after the incident, Buckley claimed that Cora had appeared in tears and apologized for her actions. He then claimed he had gone to her house earlier in the day to get some of his clothes, and when he showed up she threatened to shoot him and threw some of his things in the street. She demanded he leave, which he did. He decided to go back and see her, but he knew she was hot tempered so he took his gun, thinking it would deter her from acting out. Buckley claimed that when she opened the door and saw him, Cora snatched the revolver from the man standing with her and shot at him. He claimed he shot at her in self-defense. The paper reported, "We do not wish to prejudice the minds of the public either for or against the prisoner, but none who know him will say he is of a quarrelsome or vindictive nature; while on the other hand, she was one of the worst of her sex. She was smart, intelligent, well educated, and good looking. Time and again, since in this county, she has been heard to say, while flourishing her knife and pistol, 'I have made many a man sick at the stomach.'"[132]

Cora died within one and one-half hours of her shooting. As she was dying, she stated her maiden name was Conway and her father was a junk dealer named John Conway, living at 251 Causeway Street in Boston, Massachusetts.[133] The city of Sacramento showed just how they felt about Cora when they posted her death notice—she was listed as a cyprian under the death notices in the Sacramento paper. In May 1874, Buckley was convicted of murder in the second degree. He was sent to San Quentin to serve a ten-year sentence.

The New Evangel

I

This is the day of the sacred strumpet,
This is the day of St. Rowdy and gang;
Ours are the tongues that triumphantly trumpet
The virtues of cut-throats in loaferly slang;
St. Mark is played out, and St. Luke's no account—
It takes our St. Bret [Harte] holy deeds to recount.

II

This is the day of the Skimpton and Bludso.
This is the day of the gambler unstained;
Roughs are like Christ, (St. John Hay has said so,)
Pardon is now by stage-thunder acts gained;
You may murder, or steal, keep a house of ill-fame;
And still go to Heaven—if you only die game!

—The Tribune, *San Luis Obispo, July 15, 1871*

3

Los Angeles and Hollywood

By the 1840s, Los Angeles was well on its way to becoming a civilized Anglican city, and the missions were being overshadowed by expansion and emigration. The region was still under Mexico's rule, but the Treaty of Guadalupe Hidalgo, signed in 1848, ceded California to the United States.

Los Angeles quickly grew as a city, and by the 1870s, trolleys, railroads, and streetcars crisscrossed the metro area. Los Angeles also made a grand showing with its oranges at the St. Louis Agricultural Fair. Grapes and other produce were getting attention as well. Parks, more rail lines, churches, and synagogues began finding their way into this burgeoning city.

Despite all the improvements, some social ills were inevitable. Brothels and prostitution had become so widespread by the 1880s that the city updated its ordinances to regulate the bawdy houses. They designated the boundaries where brothels, houses of ill fame, or bawdy houses were allowed to operate. The ordinance was quite specific, defining the area as:

> commencing at the center of High Street and New High Street, and thence southerly along New High Street to the center of Temple Street; thence westerly along the center of Temple Street to the center of Fort Street, thence southerly along the center of Fort Street to the center of Third Street; thence easterly along the center of Third Street to the center of Main Street; thence southerly along the center of Main Street to the center of Mayo Street; thence easterly along the center of Mayo Street to the center of Los Angeles Street; thence northerly along the center of Los Angeles Street to the center of First Street; thence along the center of First Street easterly to a point 200 feet east of the east line of Alameda Street; thence northerly parallel with Alameda Street to its intersection with a prolongation of center line of High Street.

Furthermore, brothels could not be in a one-story house, in a basement, or on the first floor of any building. If these businesses became a nuisance or violated any of the provisions, then the owner would be charged with a misdemeanor. Penalties included fines of up to $200, six months in jail, or a combination of the two.[134] By the 1890s, Los Angeles' population was just over 50,000.[135]

Los Angeles continued to grow, and by the early 1910s the motion picture industry was taking root. Hollywood would soon follow. It was into this melting pot of people, industry, and agriculture that many madams found an eager clientele.

GUSSIE OR JESSIE BLAND, AKA MRS. DEFOREST

Gussie Bland was a madam who had establishments in both San Francisco and later in Los Angeles. This "American adventuress," as the media of the day called her, made national news—in 1887 Gussie Bland's name appeared in newspapers across the nation.

This adventurer, under the name of Mrs. DeForest, made her way to Shanghai, China, in April 1886, where she met Englishman William

Hogg Wolseley Markham. Markham was the assistant paymaster for the British war vessel HMS *Espoir* while cruising off the coast of China. He was supposed to have sailed on the *Espoir* for the Yucatan, but he actually stayed in Shanghai where he met the lovely Gussie. He, like so many others, fell for a beautiful wanton woman. Gussie became "infatuated" with William when she learned of his large "income." Markham stole $13,000 while he was aboard the *Espoir* by forging the ship commander's name on requisitions for cash.

Markham spent lavishly to show his affection and impress her. Within a short time, Gussie was given $6,500 in bank notes for the Hongkong and Shanghai Banking Corporation. She then purchased a note from the Oriental Bank of Shanghai for $1,000 under the name of Goardine (or Jourdeane) and gave it to Markham. The two lived like rich lovers for a while, but then Markham suspected that his forgery had been discovered and he boarded the SS *City of Sydney* on April 30, 1886, intending to elude officials. Thinking a disguise would help, he shaved his beard and moustache and donned a pair of blue sunglasses.[136] Detective John Coffey and Officer Christopher Cox were also on the steamer in pursuit of another criminal when they became suspicious of Markham. Markham was en route to San Francisco to meet up with Gussie, who departed on the next ship after Markham's. When he arrived in San Francisco, Markham checked into the Russ House under the name William Cordina. When he learned the Pinkertons were in pursuit, he headed to Kansas City, Missouri, where he lived modestly, working as an insurance company agent. But Captain Lee of the San Francisco police department, along with others, were still in pursuit of Markham.

Gussie had settled back into her saloon and brothel business at 128 North Alameda Street. One of her frequent customers was Charles Rich, and when he wasn't in town, he had his mail delivered to him in care of Gussie. One of the detectives watching the brothel saw a letter that had been mailed from Kansas City to Rich. The Pinkerton agents visited Gussie's brothel and opened a bottle of wine. After she imbibed too much, she told them about her British beau who was living in Kansas City as Luke Charles Rich. She felt no need to protect Markham and even ridiculed him by saying that he was just a soft

Englishman who had stupidly thrown all his money away on her and he was still infatuated with her.[137] Gussie's flowing words allowed the Pinkertons and Captain Lee to formulate a plan to catch Markham. Once they discovered the address where Markham was living, Captain Lee sent a decoy letter. It was addressed to Luke Charles Rich, the name that Markham had assumed in Kansas City. When he called for the letter, Markham was arrested.[138] The British government quickly demanded his extradition, and a warrant to do so was issued on July 21, 1887. Finally out of options, Markham confessed to the forgery charges and was eventually handed over to British authorities for trial in Hong Kong. According to the December 26, 1887, edition of the *Internal Revenue Record and Customs Journal*, Markham pleaded guilty on October 21 to embezzling a total of $10,000. He was sentenced to "five years' imprisonment with hard labor."

All that's left to tell about Gussie is that she began her career in Los Angeles, went to San Francisco for a while, and returned to Los Angeles in 1887. In 1888, she was still living on Alameda Street—supposedly with a gambler. From there, she disappeared from the historical record.

Sylvia Daniels

Sylvia Daniels, who sometimes went by the name Silva, was born on a December day in Mississippi during the mid- to late 1850s. It's not known when or how Sylvia arrived in Los Angeles, but she struggled to earn an honest living as a hard-working laundrywoman and later seesawed between that and being a madam. In her lifetime, or at least until she was in her fifties, Sylvia gave birth to seven children. Only one survived. She claimed to have had a younger sister named Eliza Washington, who was unmarried and born in Texas. She also claimed to be the widow of George Daniels. Oddly, according to records, Sylvia's parents were born in Mississippi, but Eliza's parents were born in Texas.

Her first son, Levi L., was born in January 1877 in Mississippi, and another son, Eddie Randolph, was born in California in February 1893. By early 1895, Sylvia was living in Los Angeles and earning a living as a laundress at 600½ New High Street. During her time in Los

Angeles, she moved up and down High Street. This was in a neighborhood known as "Sonoratown" where a large Mexican and African population resided. By 1896, she had relocated to 614½ New High, where she shared a home with fellow washerwoman Bertha Krigler, who was also of African descent. Something happened between the women and at the end of March, Sylvia accused Bertha of cutting her clotheslines that held freshly laundered items.[139]

By August 11, 1897, Sylvia had given up the laundry business and was arrested for keeping a disorderly house on New High Street called the Buena Vista. She was arrested by Officer Talamantes on a warrant that had been sworn out earlier in the week. Sylvia's den of iniquity was a place where some of the worst class of characters in town visited and brawls occurred nightly.[140] She was taken to jail to await her fate and demanded a trial by jury, which was set for August 18. In September, she was tried on a charge of vagrancy and ordered to pay a fine of $25. The *Los Angeles Herald* referred to her as "A Notorious Woman. Sylvia Daniels, the colored siren who keeps a house of ill fame."[141] Apparently a small fine like $25 was not enough to slow her down, and she dodged a similar charge in November when Judge Morrison dismissed the case before it went to trial.

In June 1900, Sylvia was back at being a laundrywoman, residing at 629 New High Street. Her sons Levi and Eddie lived with her at this time. There was also a Texas-born janitor named John Williams living there, who may have been Sylvia's paramour. For the next four years, Sylvia did her laundry and ironing at 624 New High Street, while her sister Eliza was just down the street at 515 New High. Sylvia, like many madams of the day, changed her marital status often. While she was still at the same address, she listed herself in a business directory as the widow of Mr. Randolph, who was Eddie's father. Then, in 1909, Sylvia had become the widow of John. The following year Sylvia, her son, and Eliza were all living at 624 New High. Sylvia and Eliza did laundry, while her son drove a wagon. She also again stated she was the widow of John, who was likely the John Williams she had previously lived with.

Sylvia's exit from Los Angeles is as mysterious as her entrance, and the 1910 census is the last known trace of her.

Lee Francis, aka Beverly Davis

Before Heidi Fleiss became known as Hollywood's most famous madam, that title was held by Lee Francis. She was the original Hollywood madam who had brothels in all the best neighborhoods from the 1920s to the 1940s. Lee's houses were top notch, sophisticated, and elegant. Her girls were inspected by a doctor twice a week, and secrecy was her specialty—well, that and a few other things, too. As a madam, Lee rarely entertained clients herself, saying she would not take customers away from her girls. And while she did take fifty percent of their fee, her guys and gals kept any tips they earned. Business was business to Lee.

Lee's life as a madam and prostitute is very well documented because of her books, but who Lee Francis really was remains a mystery. While her true birth name is not known, she claims she was born to French immigrants in 1895 in San Francisco under the name of "Isabelle Dubois." San Francisco, like the rest of the country, was having a grand old time during the Gay Nineties. Lee wrote about this in one of her books: "Red-light districts were called the abomination. They stank of evil stinks. Ministers of the Gospel ruled the fireside and women prayed. Ladies kept their ankles from appearing in public and emoted behind high corsets."[142] Her life story appeared in two books—one was titled *Call House Madam* and was written by Serge Wolsey in 1942 on her behalf. The other book was called *Ladies on Call* and was published in 1965. That book was later rereleased as *Hollywood Madam* in 1987. Lee authored the two latter books herself and mostly reported actual names and places.

In the first book, *Call House Madam*, Lee claimed her mother was in love with another man before an arrangement had been made with her father. Her mother's parents thought the man she loved had no future, so they arranged a marriage with this new man. Her mother was forced to marry a French physician who was twenty-two years her senior. They had five children, with Lee being the youngest. According to Lee, her mother nicknamed her after her true love and her father resented Lee for it. When she was six years old, he decided that Lee was in need of reform and sent her to St. Mary's convent in Los Angeles. Since Lee used false names, it's impossible to know if she truly attended St. Mary's Academy on 21st Street, or the Convent of the Immaculate Heart of Mary on West Pico, or perhaps a different convent in another town. Regardless, Lee's mother had no say in the matter of shipping her youngest off to a convent, but she was devastated by their separation.[143]

Lee donned the convent's gray uniform with red piping and white collar and spent eight tedious years with the holy sisters. She watched as other children's parents visited, and Lee couldn't understand why she never received a letter or a visit from her mother because they were so close. When the girl who normally delivered the convent mail got sick, the fourteen-year-old Lee got her chance to learn what really happened. A sister asked Lee to deliver the mail instead. At first, it saddened her to see all the letters from mothers to their children, but her heart palpitated when she saw her mother's beautiful blue, square stationery. It wasn't addressed to her, but to the Mother Superior. This seemed odd to Lee, so she opened the letter. In it, Lee's mother inquired as to what had happened to her child. She discovered that her father had instructed Mother Superior to prevent all communication between Lee and her mother for both their sakes.

With all the anger of a young, betrayed teenager, Lee began planning her escape to Sacramento and to the return address on the letter. The fourteen-year-old Lee had no money, but she desperately boarded a train with little more than hope. It was on this trip where Lee met the woman who would forever change her destiny. In the beginning, Lee believed her meeting of the wealthy looking "Hilda Fernald" was a stroke of good fortune. She would soon learn otherwise. Hilda took pity on this poor girl who was clearly an escapee from a convent—her uniform gave her away. Hilda befriended Lee and paid for her ticket. She also assured Lee that she would get her to her brother's house, which is where she was hoping to find her mother. Lee asked Hilda why she was helping her, and Hilda told Lee of a time in her life when she needed help and was now repaying the favor. As promised, she took Lee to her brother's house, asked for the phone number, and went on her way.

When Lee excitedly arrived at her brother's house, she soon learned that her *maman* was already gone. A saddened but still hopeful Lee decided to stay with her brother and his wife until they could reach their mother. Unfortunately for Lee, her sister-in-law treated her like a slave and gave her every nasty, dirty chore she could think of. When Lee told her brother about what she was enduring, he replied that he was helpless and told Lee to make the best of it. After a couple of months, Lee couldn't take it anymore and made up her mind to leave. At that moment, the phone rang. Lee desperately hoped it was her mother, but was disappointed when she heard Mrs. Fernald's voice. Not that Lee didn't like Hilda, but she longed for her mother. Lee spoke with her new friend and told her about her sister-in-law and what she was enduring. Hilda once again came to Lee's rescue and told her she would come get Lee and help her.

Lee, needing help and seeing no harm in trusting a woman who had helped her before, went with Hilda. She took Lee to meet a sixty-year-old-man she called Colonel Dashfield. At first, Lee was cautious, but the Colonel bought her expensive bonbons, candy, and other items, and she warmed to him. He and Hilda then took Lee to an expensive hotel where they had dinner. Lee recalled it was romantic and fun and she was even offered a cocktail at dinner. The next morning Lee woke up in the Colonel's bed feeling "very sore down there." All she could remember was Hilda and the Colonel offering her that drink at dinner. The Colonel had returned to the room while she was sleeping, bringing her pretty lingerie and other clothes, and she thought it all very dreamy.

They told her to stay in the hotel and to keep the door locked at all times. Hilda and the Colonel primed and spoiled Lee for three months as they whisked her off to the theater, dinners, and more. Hilda and the Colonel had to formulate a quick plan when they soon learned that Lee had become pregnant with the Colonel's child. On top of that, Lee's brother was hunting for her. Before he could find her, Hilda took Lee to a hospital where she became "no longer pregnant." The Colonel's lawyers showed up at the hospital and gave Lee a check for $10,000 if she swore not to speak about what had happened. Lee took the payment, but this wasn't the end of the scheme that Hilda and the Colonel had planned for Lee. Despite everything, years later Lee remembered the Colonel fondly. She wrote, "As a youngster just out of school, I became the spoiled darling of a doting old man."[144]

Around 1909, they shuttled Lee down to San Francisco and set her up with one of the highest-class madams of the time, a voluptuous redhead who Lee called Jessie Sherman. In reality, this was Jessie Hayman, aka Diamond Jessie, known for her lavish parlors and girls. Lee's $10,000 hush money was turned over to Jessie, who gladly accepted the petite lass into her fold. Of the $10,000, Lee had to spend about $6,000 for an extensive entertainment wardrobe. Lee was required to purchase a fox fur for suits, tailored suits, street dresses, dress coats, twelve pairs of street shoes, four and a half dozen hose, six pocketbooks, two evening bags, street and evening gloves, evening gowns, negligees, teddy slips, twenty-four nightgowns, evening wraps, evening shoes, mules (slip-on shoes), handkerchiefs, and blouses.[145]

It was at Jessie's 130 Eddy Street brothel where the four-foot, eleven-inch, fourteen-year-old Lee became Violet Adair. It was also here where Lee received her "education" and learned to become a madam. She stayed with Jessie for about two years, and then a "Mr. Ellerton" approached her about starting her own brothel. Lee claimed she was barely sixteen. Jessie Sherman was retiring soon and not only approved of Lee's new venture, but supported her with money and clients, just down the street from Jessie. When she opened her brothel, Violet Adair became Lee Francis. By 1915, she had her own brothel on the top floor of an apartment hotel at 144 Eddy. It was called the Empress Hotel. The Empress was opened in 1911; it was a modern establishment newly furnished with furniture of birds-eye maple, mahogany, and walnut, along with velvet and Axminster carpets imported from Britain. Quality mattresses, steam heat, hot water, and private phones were installed in each room. The girls' rooms that had private baths rented for $1 per day or $5 per week.[146]

Lee was doing well at her new venture until 1917, when Reverend Paul Smith began traveling up and down the Pacific Coast, convincing cities, including San Francisco, to clamp down on vice. Lee was cautioned to close her doors. She did, but she stayed in the area for a year or so, and then went to Reno, Nevada, where she met a friend she called Nora. The two soon left Reno and landed in Los Angeles where they took an apartment together. Lee claims she arrived in Los Angeles in 1929, but some of her book timelines would put her there sooner. She soon married a man named John Ogden Francis and they lived on Rampart Street for two years. John asked Lee to give up the brothel business and she agreed. While she was married to Francis, she became a well-respected member of several country clubs with her husband. Unfortunately, her husband did not earn a steady living. Lee grew tired of supporting him and filed for divorce.

After that, Lee was introduced to a Los Angeles politician named Charles H. Crawford. During the 1920s, Crawford's loosely organized crime syndicate was known as the City Hall Gang. He always set Lee up in posh palaces all around the proper areas of Hollywood, where the best clients played. He didn't do it for free, and Lee paid him his cut and never had a problem with the police. Crawford was tightly connected to Hollywood. Some of Lee's customers included Jean Harlow, who she said liked both men and women and her sex very rough. She once set a bed on fire in Lee's brothel to make things more exciting. She also deeply scratched the inside thighs of one of Lee's best girls, who refused to service Harlow after that. Another client, Errol Flynn, was also known to get very violent after drinking. Lee made a point of noting that the rumors of Clark Gable visiting her brothel were totally untrue. She wrote that he ". . . was a good friend, but never set foot in my place."[147]

One of Lee's first brothels from Crawford was a luxurious home on Rossmore Street, near the Wilshire Country Club. She also operated out of multiple locations around L.A. to avoid being caught in a raid. By the early 1900s, parlor houses could be found in residential areas as well as known prostitution districts. Lee wrote, "Segregation of parlor houses is largely a thing of the past. Underworld districts still exist. Tenderloins. But my call houses are in the best neighborhoods."[148] Lee's good fortune ran out when Crawford was murdered in a gangster hit in May 1931. She then had to start paying as many as three different "bosses" to keep her out of trouble.

By the late 1930s, Lee was ready to quit the business and open her own legitimate nightclub on the Sunset Strip. She invested heavily and named her place Club Versailles. She created a business entity

Jean Harlow kissing Senator Robert Reynolds, 1937. PHOTOGRAPH COURTESY OF THE LIBRARY OF CONGRESS, LC-DIG-HEC-22087.

so her madam name wasn't associated with the club. But the men who wanted her to stay in the madam business made sure that she couldn't get her liquor license. Lee was infuriated and was forced back into being a madam, but she had already turned over her call girl list to her best girl, Celia. The redheaded Celia set up her own palatial brothel on "La Reina Drive" in the Santa Monica hills, but Lee took it over after Club Versailles failed. She was back to being Hollywood's madam, the best at ensuring privacy for her movie stars, executives, and more. In the 1930s, she moved to her last location, the Hacienda Arms at 8439 Sunset Boulevard. The Hacienda became the Coronet around 1939 and was later dubbed "House of Francis." It remains on the Hollywood tours today.[149]

Toward the latter part of the 1930s, Lee retired and opened a small nightclub on Beverly Boulevard, simply named The Club. Lee thought she was finally free from her life of vice, so she began writing

The House of Francis, which housed Lee Francis's brothel, on Sunset Boulevard.
PHOTOGRAPH COURTESY LOS ANGELES WIKIMEDIA COMMONS, CC BY-SA 3.0.

her memoirs with an author named Serge Wolsey. In all her years as a madam, Lee was never arrested, thanks to her strategic and congenial relationships with local law enforcement. It also didn't hurt that, early on, she learned to stay in their good graces by serving them French champagne and Russian caviar when they came to inquire. Some also got to "visit" with her girls. All of that came to an end in 1940, when Lee was arrested on a trumped-up morals charge and spent the month of April behind bars. Lee reasoned she was framed because she was working on a tell-all book called *Call House*. Lee's clients were high-profile politicians, celebrities, and business moguls, and they were worried she might reveal names. They had forgotten about Lee's code of conduct and abandoned her when she needed their help.

The original title to her book was *Call House*, but "Madam" was later added. *Call House Madam* was first published in 1942, but Lee received no credit or even a mention in the book. Serge Wolsey had convinced Lee that using her real name or the names of anyone else could land her in serious legal trouble. He advised her to change the names and places of everything in the book and she agreed. In the book, Lee Francis became Beverly "Bee" Davis. Jessie Hayman

Lee Francis and Judge Cecil Holland, 1940. PHOTOGRAPH COURTESY OF THE UNIVERSITY OF CALIFORNIA, LOS ANGELES, CHARLES E. YOUNG RESEARCH LIBRARY.

became Jessie Sherman. Club Versailles became Club Marseilles and so on. The aliases didn't stray too far from the truth, but it was enough to throw most people off the trail.

In 1945, before the book was released, Lee filed a $750,000 lawsuit against Serge Wolsey and the publisher, Martin Tudordale, Inc. She claimed that Wolsey stole her story and refused to give her any portion of the profits.[150] The newspaper reported that Wolsey paid some of Lee's girls for the information. Lee did not win the case.

On April 24, 1945, before the book was released, the U.S. Postmaster General barred it from being sent through the mail because it was "undesirable," a euphemism for obscene. When the book was finally released, it was considered scandalous, and book agents were arrested for distributing and selling the book. In 1946, Hollywood book distributor Marcel Rodd was named in a secret grand jury indictment. He was charged with sending 100 copies of the book through the mail from New York to San Diego.[151] A few months later, a newspaper in Pennsylvania reported that Hollywood was bracing for a sensational censored exposé written by Lee Francis. In 1947, the court ruled on Marcel Rodd's case, and he was levied a $2,500 fine for handling an obscene book in interstate commerce. The court declared that *Call House Madam* was obscene, lewd, and lascivious and filthy.[152] On May 11, 1948, the *L.A. Times* reported that Rodd petitioned the U.S. Supreme Court to hear his case but was denied. That court stated that the book was repulsive. It's likely the justices ruled this way because Lee went into graphic detail about the sexual customs she witnessed when she visited foreign countries as she looked for new ways to entertain her more difficult clients. She also included language and ideas that were shocking for the 1940s. For example, in describing San Francisco in the 1890s, she wrote, "Breasts were simply heaving bosoms that artificial emotion moved up and down at a given signal. That the breasts and nipples of a woman were centers of pleasure in performing the sex act, only an evil-minded prostitute might admit it—but a lady? Never! Not even if at some unguarded moment she got wise to the effect."[153]

It took seven years and another printing, but by 1957, the book was back in bookstores all over the country. The book was so popular that in 1960, the Hertz-Lyon Productions company announced it was doing a film on the best-selling book. By this time, Lee had been happily out of the business for many years and was managing an apartment hotel in Los Angeles.[154] According to the 1987 reprint of the book, Lee passed away in March 1966. Since her true identity is not known, the details of her death are lost . . . for now.

4

Fresno

The town of Fresno is a hub in the San Joaquin Valley. It got a late start in comparison to many of California's other pioneer towns. In 1856, Fresno County was formed out of Buena Vista and Tulare Counties. The area contained 14,000 cattle, 1,400 horses, 500 oxen, 200 mules, 4,000 swine, 1,000 sheep, and 560 goats. There were also two vineyards, three ferries, three steam sawmills, and one artesian well. In 1860, the first telegraph wires were strung, and in 1870, the discovery of a grove of 400-foot-tall sequoia trees sparked the logging industry. By that time, the population was about 6,300 people, and in 1872, the town of Fresno was incorporated.[155]

Toward the end of the 1870s, Fresno had its own newspaper, livery stables, livery and feed stores, blacksmiths, attorneys, hotels, and just about anything else one needed or wanted. Brothels came under the wanted column. Fresno officials and residents alike knew there were madams and prostitutes in their town. In 1888, they passed an ordinance that prohibited loud noises or shouting on the streets and

Fresno in 1909. PHOTOGRAPH COURTESY OF THE LIBRARY OF CONGRESS, PAN US GEOG - CALIFORNIA NO. 27
(F SIZE) [P&P].

required that the doors and windows of houses of ill fame be kept closed day and night. If anyone was caught breaking this ordinance, they could be fined between $10 and $50, or spend between five and fifty days in jail, or both.[156]

By 1889, Fresno's demimonde was causing angst for many, and an anonymous letter appeared in the *Daily Morning Republican*. The writer simply signed their name "Virtue." They said that in addition to the bawdy houses on the other side of the tracks, there were three "varieties" operating in the proper section of town. They also stated there were public dens where business was openly conducted with no attempt to hide what they were and held women with no respectability. Their clothes and appearance immediately gave them away, not to mention their calls on the street. "Virtue" wrote, "A person entering their dens does so with full knowledge of his situation, and should be responsible for the consequences. This class makes no pretentions to respectability, and any person contaminating himself with such associates is inexcusable and deserves no sympathy." They claimed there were at least twelve to eighteen of these dens in Fresno that housed over sixty "inmates."

The letter writer next targeted the lodging houses and their residents. "Virtue" noted that not all were bad, and they didn't care who took offense. They stated that there were "lady lodgers" whom they called "chippies." They also claimed these were the worst, because

they made themselves appear respectable with their clothes, appearance, and manners. The writer claimed there was hardly a block in Fresno's business section that didn't have this class of occupant. They believed there were as many as fifty to seventy-five women prostitutes pretending to be proper ladies.

The last class that "Virtue" noted were the blackmailers. They claimed these were the worst of them all, because once a tempted man fell prey to such a woman, she would own him. "Virtue" closed their letter with "This is the element that should be driven to its proper place. They should be exposed and rooted out of society for she it is that is most to be feared who wears the gilded cloak to conceal her crimes."[157]

Let's meet the ladies and madams of Fresno.

MAY E. ELLIS

May Ellis was one of the women who "Virtue" had written about in the paper. She arrived in Fresno around early 1889 and had come from Chicago with a nice bank account. May's time in Fresno may have been brief, but it was memorable.

When she arrived in Fresno, May booked a room in the local hotel and began making inquiries about buying a house. Property man about town E. A. Pattison heard May was looking for a house and called on her at the hotel. She appeared to be a very proper lady and told Pattison she was a married woman whose husband was in San Francisco at the time. Pattison had no reason to question

May's word, so he proceeded to show her several homes. When they arrived at a white cottage in town on M Street, May knew it was exactly what she was looking for and made arrangements with Pattison to buy it. They agreed that May would pay $2,400 upfront and then monthly installments of $100 until it was paid off. They drew up a contract and Pattison went away thinking he had a made a terrific deal.

May moved into her white cottage on M Street and brought in her girls. Within six weeks of her purchase, May's house had gained a bad reputation.[158] Once the town realized who had moved into their residential neighborhood, they wanted her gone. They soon found out it would be difficult to get her to move since May had purchased the house. Most madams simply rented a place. When the townspeople learned of the contract Pattison signed with May, they became anxious. It was bad enough that Ellis had a brothel in town, but that it was located across the street from the new brick high school being built was an outrage. May's place was on M Street, but it could not be mistaken for a simple house because of her particular form of advertisement. She placed a red translucent cloth over the white glass transom above the doors. When the rays of the flickering coal lamp lit it up, a ruby-hued glow was exuded. Some people were so angered that they demanded May and her nymphs du pave be moved to Chinatown or even out of town completely.

The local paper reported that on two nights in June during the Merchant's carnival, about a dozen men left their female escorts to spend an hour or more "basking in the fascinations of the nymphs du pave who have given the white cottage on M a reputation of infamy." Their Victorian outrage continued, "With the kisses of harlots yet moist upon their lips these men have returned to the carnival to escort their innocent and unsuspecting charges home."[159]

When customers knocked upon May's cottage door, they were greeted by a tall, voluptuous blonde in black Spanish lace that clung to her figure. Once they stepped inside, they were greeted by Jane Doe and Sallie Roe, two exquisitely dressed young women who were ready to entertain. Customers enjoyed beer and wine and indulged in saucy conversation until they were too drunk to talk.

The *Republican* began a crusade to get May out of her M Street abode and into Chinatown. First, they brought up the fact that she was selling unlicensed liquor from her brothel. When she started her business, May applied for and was granted a state license to sell liquor at her place of business as a retail liquor dealer. She failed, however, to get a license from the town of Fresno because it would've cost a prohibitive $150 per month. A license for selling liquor at places other than a brothel was a mere $20 per quarter. A trial was set in June, but it was thought she would relocate to Chinatown before her court date.[160]

Second, they ran multiple newspaper stories so the local authorities couldn't ignore it. City Marshal Baker told the *Republican* that if anyone filed a complaint with his office about the house of ill fame, then he would be obligated to do his duty. In mid-June, one of May's neighbors, W. J. Lowery, did just that. He appeared before Justice Wolcott to file a complaint.

As the judge listened to Lowery, he quickly realized action was needed and he issued an arrest warrant for May and her girls. When they were presented with the warrant, May remained aloof, but her girls were nervous because they had never been arrested before. May donned a black silk dress and a dark straw hat that was adorned with pale green leaves and ribbons. The brunette Jane Doe, whose real name was Alice Compton, also slipped into a black silk dress and a white linen embroidered sack. Blonde Sallie Roe, who was actually named Montie Ruggles, wore a tight-fitting light brown dress. The women were taken to attorney W. D. Grady's office so May could get a bond while awaiting trial. When the attorney tried to be flip with the judge, claiming that these women lived in a respectable part of town and were no risk, the judge didn't like it. Grady suggested a bond of $25 per woman, but the judge said no, so Grady offered $50. The judge settled on $200 for May and $100 for each of her girls. The *Republican* reported that it had a "trump" card it would play if May didn't move her brothel.[161]

On July 11, May appeared before Judge Wolcott and begrudgingly agreed to move to Chinatown. She was fined $6.60, plus court costs, for keeping a house of ill fame on M Street. The judge said the fine was minimal because she had complied with the demands of the people.

Alice Compton and Montie Ruggles were fined the same amount.[162] That night, May and her girls dressed in their nightgowns and slid into their new beds in their Chinatown brothel. They were abruptly awakened about 3:30 A.M. by their Chinese cook yelling "fire!" The flames were engulfing their building, so May jumped from the second-story front porch in her night clothes and suffered bruises and a spinal injury. A new girl named Frankie leapt from a window and was severely injured, with cuts to her lip and breast. Montie Ruggles also jumped out a window and sustained bruises and cuts, but she was not severely injured. Lastly was Alice Compton, who slid down one of the balcony posts and badly damaged her hands and lost the skin of her palms. May lost all her furniture, which was valued at $1,500. May's cook, who saved the women's lives, jumped from the window and broke his leg.[163]

The cause of the fire was disputed. Some claimed that men were carelessly smoking opium and knocked over a lantern, while others said an explosive was placed in the hallway of May's brothel. It was also reported that the fire was started in an attempt to burn May Ellis and her girls to death. Flames ravaged several buildings before it was put out. It destroyed one-third of Chinatown, with a monetary loss of $20,000 to $30,000. May wanted the city to allow her to move back to her house on M Street so she could recover. If they wouldn't allow that, then she requested that someone care for her in the local hospital. Because of her connections, she was given one of the best doctors in town and was soon on the mend.[164]

May quickly recovered and proved to be a feisty woman in her town despite what people thought of her. When the owner of the *Republican*, Shanklin, verbally attacked May in the paper, she returned the favor physically. On August 1, 1889, May met Shanklin at his lawyer's office, where she slapped him and then knocked him down with her bare hands.[165] This may have been May's last act in Fresno because May E. Ellis seems to have vanished into history soon afterward.

ALMA JEWETT

George and Elizabeth Parish Jewett arrived in California by 1868, staying first in Eel River in Humboldt County. In 1870, they moved to Golden City, Tuolumne County, where George worked as a quartz miner. Alma Luella and her three sisters were all born in California, and she was the second daughter, born in April 1873. Her sisters included an older girl named Minnie and a younger sister named Sadie, who was an artist. It's interesting to note that Alma and her sister Sadie switched birth years and ages when they participated in the government's periodic censuses. Even their death records show each other's dates. Alma's father grew up in a large family in Antwerp, New York, and Alma's grandfather's name was Liberty Jewett. By 1880, George Jewett had given up mining and had become a watchman, while Alma's mother stayed at home like most women of her time. Alma, on the other hand, had made her way to Fresno by 1889.

The town was growing, and early in 1889, the manager of the Farmers Bank, Mr. Phillips, erected a two-story building at 1027 J Street. This was Mr. Phillips's personal investment property; he wanted a convenient location for his prospective tenant so he chose the center of town between Mariposa and Fresno Streets. Phillips leased the building to S. H. Williams & Son to operate undertaking parlors for three years. Williams had settled in and opened his parlors when a very respectable and ladylike Alma approached him. Young Alma offered letters of introduction and told Williams that she had just arrived from San Francisco and wanted to rent the upper floor for lodgings and an art gallery. It seems Alma was using her sister's artistic talent as her own. Williams had no reason to suspect Alma had something else in mind, so with Phillips's permission, he sublet the second floor to her for $50 per month for one year. Just to be sure, Williams sent his son Ed around town to see if anyone knew Alma. Either he didn't ask the right people, or no one told him she was an inmate of May Ellis's white cottage bagnio on M Street.

When the "Rooms to Let" sign went up in early 1889, no one thought that Alma would be opening a brothel. She not only had a brothel, which she called the Birdcage, but she also sold alcohol to her customers without a liquor license. Most of the city was outraged once they learned what Alma was doing. The *Fresno Weekly Republican* decided to go after Alma's Birdcage with a full-on written assault. In July 1889, funeral parlor owner S. H. Williams commended the paper for their efforts. He wrote, "I am glad and thankful that the Republican has begun to fight to drive out those lewd women upstairs. I have tried to get her out before, but she has a year's lease and defies me to expel her." He was frustrated that the police couldn't get her to go either. Alma was overheard telling someone that Williams was going to have a hard time getting her out. Williams, being an abiding Baptist, was of course distraught and refused to give up. He threatened to place a man at the door and write down the names of every man who entered her parlors, in case he needed to use them as witnesses.[166]

Just a few days later, Alma once again found herself the topic of the *Weekly Republican*. This time, she was a witness against J. W. Shanklin, owner of the *Republican*, and John P. Cosgrove, his editor, who were accused of conspiring against their competitor. (Shanklin was the same man who drove May Ellis out of her M Street cottage and into Chinatown.) C. B. Horton of the *Evening Expositor* claimed the men attempted to frame him for solicitation and committing a felony. Horton had a signed affidavit from Alma who swore that Shanklin paid her $20 to frame Horton, and in exchange, they would stop trying to shut down her business. Their plan was for Alma and Horton to meet at a restaurant where Shanklin and Cosgrove would be waiting to overhear the conversation. The plan fell through; Horton didn't go to the restaurant and instead sent word to Alma that he would only meet her at his office.[167] The case was soon dismissed because the judge stated that no crime was noted in the complaint.[168]

When the *Republican*'s plan against its competitor failed, all bets were off, and they renewed their attacks on Alma in the summer of 1889. The *Republican* had just successfully forced May Ellis's bagnio out of town and were now focusing their full attention on Alma's Birdcage. The newspaper wrote an editorial about it with the hope that she would close her business and just leave. That wasn't Alma's style. Two of her girls did get nervous; they packed their trunks and left. Afterward, Alma asked to have an interview with two of the reporters from the *Republican*. With all the sincerity she could muster, she told them she had dismissed all her girls and was turning her business into a legitimate boarding house. Alma was quite convincing and satisfied the reporters with her sincerity. However, they soon realized they had been duped and began an investigation. They placed someone across the street to observe the goings-on. A subsequent story in the *Republican* remarked that there must have been over 150 rooms on the second floor because of all the people who entered. They also commented that these same people must live at more than one house, because they stayed only for an hour or so and then left.

Finally, the newspaper sent an investigator into the building. He saw yellow letters on a black background tin sign with the words "furnished rooms." The investigator turned the doorknob, walked up the stairs, and pushed an electric bell that sounded an alarm. It summoned Miss Alma, a tall, shapely brunette. As he entered one of her four elegant parlors, she invited him to "visit" with her "children," as Alma called them, odd considering that at the time, she was only sixteen herself. The investigator noted that during a thirty-minute period, no fewer than thirty customers had entered the house. They could choose from two brunettes named Lulu and Flossie, or a blonde named Annie. Once the girls started to mingle, drinks were ordered and charged at regular saloon rates of $0.12½ per glass. Clients could choose from beer, whiskey, gin, port, sherry, sarsaparilla, soda water, or claret. The more sophisticated clients might splurge and open a quart bottle of champagne for $5. Alma kept her liquor money in her slippers and reportedly jingled when she walked.

Because her business was so brisk, she planned to bring in two more girls from San Francisco. She also wanted extra girls because both she and her "children" were terrified of being burned in a fire like her former boss May Ellis had been. After May's fire, some of her girls moved in with Alma. Her plan worked well, and if one girl ran off, then she had a backup. It was said they stayed up all night until the sun began to rise and other people started their daily business, so if someone saw a fire, they could sound the fire alarm. When the reporter concluded his story, he noted that both Alma and her clients wanted a back staircase, though exactly why wasn't made clear. The reporter also noted that she should be moved to Chinatown and suggested that officials do their job and arrest her.[169]

On one crisp day in October, a young man hadn't finished sowing his wild oats and had become quite drunk on wine. Apparently, he grossly insulted another man in the Birdcage. This young man was quickly tossed down the stairs, but he climbed back up, only to be attacked again. His next attempt was thwarted by the young nymphs of the house, who all began to pummel him. One girl even hit him in the shin with a chair. To add insult to injury, they, too, tossed him down the luxurious imported Axminster carpet. The assumption was that no one was arrested because Alma had close connections in important places.[170]

In January 1890, the building's owner, Phillips, demanded the police or the city arrest Alma and the inmates of the house, but they had no legal grounds to do so.[171] It seemed that Phillips was aware of Alma's seedy business, but no one would accuse him of knowingly allowing a brothel to operate in his building. Some claimed that local officials had been paid off or blackmailed to look the other way. The *Republican* wrote, "The Fancy Salary [likely another brothel] and the Fancy Bird cage should both be abolished."[172]

Around the same time this was being discussed in the local paper, Alma lost one of her girls, a plump blonde named Midget, to Mrs. Brown's boarding house. But Mrs. Brown didn't benefit for very long, because young Midget's father arrived in town from his nearby Selma farm. He begged his daughter to start leading a better life and to come home. The next day, Midget boarded a northbound train and stated she would take her father's advice and was going to live with relatives. It seems Alma wasn't the only wayward girl at the Birdcage.

One of Alma's girls, Ollie Thorndyke, had a regular client who adored her. John O'Keefe, aka William Thorndyke, was Ollie's consort, and she wanted her man dressed in the finest clothes. On New Year's Day in 1890, O'Keefe and T. W. Cairns arrived to work at the Grand Central barbershop in town. Before the men-about-town arrived to have their hair and moustaches trimmed for the holiday, O'Keefe noticed that Cairns was sporting a $120 diamond pin on his jacket. Cairns left the pin in his jacket pocket when the men removed their jackets in a private room and changed into their barber whites. O'Keefe wanted that pin and lifted it later when Cairns wasn't looking. Because it was in his pocket, Cairns didn't miss it right away and O'Keefe ran off to Oakland. The Fresno police contacted Ollie, who was corresponding with her paramour, and a decoy letter was sent to O'Keefe in Oakland. Fresno's finest also sent a letter to the local Oakland police and asked them to arrest a man at the post office picking up a letter for William Thorndyke or John O'Keefe. The police were happy to do so, except that O'Keefe was already in their jail because he had stolen another man's jacket and vest. After serving his eight-day jail term, he was shipped back to Fresno to be tried for larceny for stealing the diamond pin.[173] A month later, Ollie was no longer working for Alma, but she was implicated in O'Keefe's diamond theft for having received stolen goods.[174] She appeared before Judge Hogue on February 11 and stated her true name was actually Mrs. John L. O'Keefe. She said she lived at Alma's Birdcage and had married O'Keefe in Mansfield, Pennsylvania, on September 2, 1886. She claimed that while living at Alma's, she had received a diamond from her husband as a New Year's gift. She did not know it was stolen. The judge took pity on Ollie and dismissed the charges.[175]

In February, Alma had her own troubles. Along with other downtown brothels, she was ordered to close down her business. A woman known as Mattie Willard once had her brothel in Chinatown, but her high-toned clients didn't like crossing the tracks at late hours. Mattie decided to make her clients happy and moved to a downtown location. Both she and Alma were being chased out by Constable Johnston. Unbeknownst to Alma, the constable had already taken his case to the grand jury because he wanted her charged with keeping a house of ill fame and for selling liquor without a license. He was asked why he hadn't arrested her in the past, and he said that Alma had threatened to say he was a regular customer, which he emphatically denied. On February 5, Johnston advised both Mattie and Alma that he had collected enough evidence to convict them of selling liquor without a license and of being inmates in houses of ill fame. He told them to move out of Fresno or at least to Chinatown.[176] But Alma refused, and Johnston was worried about her threats, so he sent Constable Morgan to arrest her, which he did. She was taken before Judge Hogue for a hearing and witnesses were summoned. Most were threatened by

Alma with the same things that Constable Johnston was—claiming that they frequented her house. Despite that, the court managed to mount a solid case, but knew with her threats and connections they could not win. Alma's attorney called for a change of venue and the case was moved to Madera. That was a great move by her attorney, because for unknown reasons, the people of Madera had a beef with the people of Fresno. They did not convict Alma Jewett, and Fresno was furious and vowed to ensure the people of Madera had good reason not to like them. Her case was dismissed on March 8, 1890.[177, 178]

Fresno officials did not relent and they continued to harass Alma. In mid-March, shortly after she was found not guilty in Madera, Constable Wofford arrested her for selling retail liquors without a license. Despite her lease being up, Alma refused to leave her second-floor residence on J Street. As before, Alma asked for a change of venue, claiming that the judge could not be fair. They finally settled on the town of Sanger. The outcome is not known, but in 1891 Alma, as an adult, was still running her house. She was yet again arrested, and this time they charged her with operating a house of ill fame. As with her past arrests, the trial was moved to Madera. Once again, the jury failed to reach a unanimous vote and Alma was not convicted.[179]

It appears that Alma's parents, like those of her former inmate Midget, had tracked her down and intervened. Her parents were also deeply religious and attended church, as did her aunts and cousins, in northern California. By March 1897, her father, George, was living at 747 Q Street, and her grandmother, Mrs. Eby, even visited in October that year. By 1898, she and her parents were living at 1533 K Street. Her father worked then as an assistant baggage manager at Valley Road. Things had really turned around by July 1898 when Alma attended a party given at Reverend Eccleston's home. She also attended another party where both men and women played games, sang, and enjoyed each other's conversation.[180]

Nevertheless, this attempt at family life didn't last long in Fresno and they headed north to Stockton. By June 1900, the twenty-seven-year-old Alma, who attended only two years of high school, was a saleswoman living with her parents, and her father was again working as a watchman. Her sister Sadie was also residing with them.

In 1909, Alma and her family visited relatives in Healdsburg, and the newspaper noted that she owned a large art store. By 1910, the family had moved to 711 North California Street, where the sisters were running their own fancy notions store. In 1916, her father died in Stockton. He had been well-known in Healdsburg, where his sister-in-law lived.[181] In 1927, Alma, her mother, and sisters Sadie and Minnie Dustin returned to Healdsburg for a visit. After their parents died, the sisters continued to run the notions store and lived in the same house well into their sixties.

Alma died on March 24, 1967, in Santa Cruz, with most people never knowing about her short stint as a madam. Neither she nor her sister Sadie ever married.

5

Mining Country

The northern California towns of Auburn, Marysville, Placerville, Dutch Flat, Tehama, and Lincoln were founded as early mining communities. It's no surprise that madams and prostitutes were found in these testosterone-filled camps. Men worked hard in cold water with their backs bent over creeks, rivers, and streams. Whiskey and women were the two things that warmed them after a hard day's work. Many of the prostitutes in these communities were Chinese women who tended to stay once they established a reputation. In contrast, Anglo women arrived and left these areas as quickly as the gold came and went.

Marysville was occupied with men who sought gold and a better life as early as the 1840s. It was named Marysville after Mary Murphy, the wife of one of the town's founders. She was a survivor of the disastrous Donner party. Marysville also had the distinction of being one of the places that Charles Boles, aka Black Bart, stayed during his bandit days. Boles told officers he had often been

Gold miners work a stream in El Dorado, circa 1850. PHOTOGRAPH COURTESY OF THE LIBRARY OF CONGRESS, LC-DIG-DS-04487.

in Marysville while on his robbery pilgrimages, but no one there ever took him for a bandit.

In the early years, towns like Marysville didn't always have their own newspapers, so their news often appeared in nearby bigger city papers. Those papers' coverage of the towns tended to be random but largely focused on the most salacious stories. When it came to prostitution, many papers tried to show the seedy side of the profession to discourage women from falling into it and to make town officials aware of the problem. An incident at a Marysville brothel served that purpose when a San Francisco paper reported that an inmate of a house of ill fame, Annie Sullivan, stabbed another, Kate Eldridge, in the shoulder. At first, everyone thought Kate would live, but then reports claimed the wound was likely fatal. Unfortunately, the papers rarely followed up on reports like these, so the outcome of this story is not known.[182]

Dutch Flat was settled by German immigrants in 1851, and it, too, had its share of prostitutes and madams. Again, most were Chinese,

The bustling Main Street of Dutch Flat in 1866. PHOTOGRAPH BY LAWRENCE & HOUSEWORTH, COURTESY OF THE LIBRARY OF CONGRESS, LC-USZ62-28974.

A freighter rolls down Main Street in Placerville, 1866. PHOTOGRAPH COURTESY OF THE LIBRARY OF CONGRESS, LC-USZ62-28142.

Businesses line Placerville's Main Street in 1866. PHOTOGRAPH COURTESY OF THE LIBRARY OF CONGRESS, LC-USZ62-20162.

but there were a few Anglo prostitutes. California native "Lizzie" was one of them. She was a twenty-five-year-old "keeping house" in Dutch Flat in 1880 with twenty-seven-year-old Mattie Howard from Connecticut, along with Nellie Axtell, who was a twenty-eight-year-old from Illinois. Not much else is known about any of these women.

Because early mining communities were so transient, men, women, and madams moved seamlessly in and out. Many of them just disappeared, much like the gold or silver dug from the ground.

MADAM MACK, AKA MRS. HANCHEN MARKS

Around 1835, a little girl was born into the world in Prussia. Her parents could never know that their little Hanchen Pflaum would become a woman of lies, deceit, and likely murder. The local papers called her a "Polish Jewess." Hanchen claimed she married Aaron Marks in San Francisco on September 8, 1856, and by 1859, they were living in Forest Hills, where she kept a house of prostitution and he ran a liquor store. She later ended the marriage by obtaining a divorce decree on April 17, 1861, in the Fourth District Court of San

Francisco. Evidence to support this appears in the *Sacramento Daily Union*, who reported that a divorce was granted in San Francisco to Hanchen Marks and Aaron Marks "on account of desertion of the wife by the husband."[183] However, other reports in late 1861 claim she had recently married an Aaron Marks who was living in California.[184] The stories told of her marriage and divorce are tangled with lies.

In 1859 Hanchen boarded a stagecoach in Forest Hills en route to Folsom. She was joined by other passengers, including an unnamed newspaper reporter. As the coach bumped and swayed along its path, the two struck up a casual conversation. Two years later, this reporter realized that his conversation with her was worthy of being retold when a sensational murder story later broke in New York City. He said the "chunky little German thing" had a smile and piercing eyes that he felt upon him as he sat directly opposite her along their jostled ride. Hanchen told him she married a man named Stamper and decided it was easier to use the name Marks rather than Stamper. She obtained a divorce from him because he deserted her when he went to Virginia City, Nevada Territory. It's possible that they used the name Stamper *instead* of Marks. She confessed to her traveling companion that she kept a brothel in Dutch Flat after her divorce, but then opened a millinery store on Third Street in Marysville. She said she also owned about $10,000 worth of real estate in Folsom. She recalled that this was about the time she decided to go East and bring her sister over from Europe.[185] How could she have divorced Marks in 1859 when she spoke with this reporter if the divorce decree shows 1861? Did the reporter mix up the details from two years ago with the current ones, or was she lying? Regardless, she was headed to Germany to get her sister.

Hanchen's younger sister, Albertina Pflaum, was born between 1834 and 1838. Hanchen joined her sister in Hamburg and the two women set sail on the steamship *Bavaria*, arriving in New York City on October 10, 1861. While on board, Albertina became involved with a forty-four-year-old married man named Sigismund Fellner. She and her married lover consummated their relationship in their cabins. Fellner's personality and good looks earned him the title "Don Juan" while on board the ship. What most passengers didn't know was that he quietly carried $50,000, most of which was in diamonds, along with him. Both Hanchen and Albertina saw the large amount of diamonds and money, perhaps during customs inspections. It was also very likely that Fellner shared this information, or even a diamond or two, with his cabin mate. Regardless of how they found out about Fellner's treasure, the sisters formed a plan. They boarded at a low house at 45 East Broadway in New York City, while Fellner took rooms at the more elegant Prescott House at 529 Broadway. Two days after Fellner checked into his room, he heard a knock on his door. When he opened it, he was greeted by Mrs. Marks, who was wielding a stiletto and demanding justice for her sister's fallen reputation. Other guests appeared from their rooms to see what was happening. According to witnesses, Fellner just wanted Marks to go away quietly, so he found what he thought was a solution.

Fellner, only being in America for a couple of days, confided in a fellow countryman named Ignatz Ratzky about what happened. When Fellner told him that "he must get out of a scrape with certain ladies who had come over to this country on the same steamer with him," Ratzky suggested that Fellner leave the Prescott and take rooms at the German boarding house at 4 Carroll Street in Brooklyn. It was here where Fellner met Mr. and Mrs. Adolph Swenzer. Fellner was a trusting soul with a large purse. Sadly, for him, he turned up dead a few days after moving into the German boarding house. His gold watch and chain, along with his money and diamonds, had all been stolen. He was found floating in the Navesink River near Applegate's Landing in Middletown, New Jersey, at the end of October, not far from a house of ill-repute. He was killed with extreme prejudice, as evidenced by the nineteen stab wounds in his heart. Police confirmed that the wounds were made with a sword cane, which was later found in Hoboken, New Jersey.[186]

Just before Fellner's body was found, Mrs. Marks and Ratzky were granted permission to access his room from the landlady. The poor landlady was convinced that Fellner had already given them permission because he was about to marry Mrs. Marks's sister. It didn't take the police long to suspect that Fellner's new rooming friends, the Swenzers, Mrs. Marks, and her sister were involved. They were promptly arrested. When police searched Albertina's room, they found Fellner's gold watch and chain. She claimed they were gifted to her by Fellner. When they searched Mrs. Marks's room, they discovered $20,000 in franc notes on the Bank of France. She claimed they were given to her by Fellner for taking liberties with her sister. Unfortunately, Fellner wasn't around anymore to substantiate or deny this. It was also reported that Mrs. Marks took $500 worth of diamonds to a jewelry store on Nassau Street to be set. The Swenzers also had two $1,000-franc notes on them, which they claimed were paid to them by Mrs. Marks as hush money. Albertina sat in jail awaiting the outcome of her charges. It must have been too much for her, because the young Albertina hung herself in her jail cell on November 2, 1861; her last words were "I am innocent, you will see. Good Bye."[187]

Mrs. Marks was escorted from her cell to her sister's, where she coldly identified the body to be that of Albertina's. Marks also claimed her sister did not commit the crime. Shortly after that, Mrs. Marks was sitting in her jail cell with a shawl wrapped around her. She, too, was on suicide watch because of the incident with her sister. No one could see what Mrs. Marks was doing under her shawl, until they saw blood. When the police got into her cell, they discovered she had sliced open the main artery on her left arm. While she lost a good deal of blood, her wound was wrapped and she lived—much to her dismay. Then, while she was en route to Freehold, New Jersey, to stand trial, she tried to jump overboard from the boat she was on, but that, too, failed. Persistent in trying to kill herself, she managed to open her wound and lost more blood while she was in the county jail. That attempt failed as well, and she survived to stand trial.[188]

As people witnessed the trial, they began to see Hanchen Marks unravel. They watched in stunned confusion as she rambled on about her dead parents and how her entire family was murdered. She also went on about how she repeatedly tried to kill herself. In the end, the judge was forced to let her go because there was not enough evidence to hold her. They did, however, convict Ratzky of murder with a life sentence on what many believed was circumstantial evidence.

After the delusional Marks was released in December, she told police she was going to Philadelphia. By the end of December, Marks was found wandering the streets of New York in a destitute condition. The Polish Jewess was taken to the local doctor for care, and reports claimed she was a raving lunatic, despondent, and incoherent. By early January, she seemed to make a full recovery and proclaimed her innocence, saying it was Ratzky who ransacked Fellner's trunk and killed him. She then returned to California, moved to Virginia City, Nevada, and then back to San Francisco.

Upon her return to California, Hanchen changed her last name to Rappapo. While she thought she had left the murder case and Fellner behind her in New York, new details of the murdered Fellner were brought to light. He was no innocent—he had fled to America after absconding with all of his wife's jewelry. A few years after the case, most believed that Ratzky was innocent and that Mrs. Marks and her sister were the real murderers.

In early 1864, Hanchen Rappapo filed a complaint against a man known as Uncle Freddy. The benevolent-looking older gentleman had refused to take her greenbacks in exchange for a note that specified gold coin had to be redeemed in gold coin. Interestingly, Hanchen was using jewelry as security against the note.[189] In October of the same year, Mrs. Rappapo was arrested for assault and battery against a Dora Marks, who was not related.[190]

By 1871, Hanchen Marks was once again running a house of prostitution in California. That tidbit was shared in one of the many newspaper stories about Ratzky, who continued to profess his innocence in the murder of "Don Juan" Fellner. His attorneys kept trying to get him released, and that would prompt reporters to recount details of the case. Ratzky served nine years in Sing Sing and then was released from prison. Hanchen may have grabbed the initial headlines in this sensational murder, but eventually she, too, faded into obscurity.

Emily Edwards-Casement, aka the Fire Queen

Placer County was home to some of the earliest gold mines, centered in the communities of Lincoln, Colfax, Roseville, and Auburn. It was here where Emily Edwards lived, operated a brothel, and died. Her brothels were neither high nor low houses but somewhere in between. Emily got her start in San Francisco, as had so many other madams.

In appearance, Emily Edwards was different—she was a free-born "quadroon," which was the term in that era for a quarter black with mixed European heritage. Emily was born in Richmond, Virginia, around 1822 and claimed to be white. Her slightly dark complexion and long, soft, jet-black hair led census takers to mark her as mulatto. Emily said her mother and father were both white, but she had no actual memory of her father because he died when she was very young. She also claimed she was a descendant of Pocahontas.[191]

In early 1850, she traveled overland and arrived in San Francisco, where she set up a saloon and dance hall. It sat on what was the old Mission Road at a location that is now Tenth and Mission Streets. In San Francisco's early days, fires were common, and on June 22, 1851, San Francisco experienced a devastating blaze just before 11 A.M. It was thought to be deliberately set and began in a frame house on Pacific Street near Powell, but strong summer sea breezes drove the flames south and east. Emily lived nearby and came to the rescue. As flames were engulfing the city, she joined the bucket brigade and also helped the hook and ladder team tear down some of the burning buildings with her bare hands. An 1855 newspaper wrote of her, "To use her own expression, 'she is a better fireman than half of the kid-glove gentry who go a-mincinly and a-cuttin' around town. . . .'"[192]

It was sometime around this incident that Emily Edwards married an Australian named Hugh Casement, Jr. She didn't know what he did for a living, but when he went to work, he traveled to 80 Battery Street near the Embarcadero. He bought his new bride a house at the corner of Eighth and Folsom Streets in 1852 but put the deed in his name only. They built a fence around the attractive little house, and she hung a sign on a large oak tree in the front offering milk punch drinks, which were her specialty.[193]

About 1853, Emily was walking along a boggy area when she noticed that a saddle horse had gotten stuck in a bog near the corner of Folsom and Johnson Streets. With no regard for herself, she jumped into the mud after male counterparts had "gin him up" according to Emily. The horse's owner, George Gordon, was so grateful for

Emily's help that he bought her new dresses and other items to show his appreciation.

Her good deeds seemed to have no end. When someone shot a cow belonging to a Mr. Russ, Emily played detective and claimed to have caught the culprit. In another incident, Marshal Seguin had laid claim to Emily's lot in South San Francisco. Rather than back down, Emily placed a chair on her flooded land, sat down, and backed up her belligerent intent with a double-barreled shotgun.[194]

Emily was very proud of her ancestral heritage and took great offense when anyone called her "colored." In 1855, she told a newspaper man, "Mr. Reporter, would you believe that I have gone through all these tribulations—known as I am to this city—always on hand at fires, ready to divide my last dollar with the poor and needed, to be called a *colored woman*!" The *Daily Alta California* reporter responded to this, writing, "We left Mrs. Edwards, sensibly impressed with her volubility and public services, and reflecting upon the mighty changes wrought in this same city of San Francisco since those troublous 'times which tried men's souls,' from '49 to '52."[195]

Emily's striking beauty, eccentric character, and odd, reckless ways brought men from all over town to her business. While she was running her brothel, her husband claimed timber land along a river and was squatting there with about eighty other men in June 1853. When the marshal arrived to serve them a summons, he was threatened, beaten, and nearly killed by a man named Holliday. Emily and Hugh lived together until 1855, when he left for his native country down under.

Emily was widely known for her charity. She, like other madams, often helped impoverished families without them knowing that a notorious madam was the one who had helped. She didn't want the attention or thanks, she just wanted to help. It was this kind-hearted nature that earned her the sobriquet of "The Fire Queen." Another great fire in November 1855 ravaged the city in the Mission Creek area where Emily's brothel was located. The Novelty Distillery, owned by James Dows & Co., was located on Mission Creek. About noon on the fateful day, the distillery's boiler exploded and scalded five men who were working inside. The spirit tanks ignited, and in a few short minutes the entire building was on fire. By the time the fire department arrived, the flames were out of control and all they could do was save the small adjoining buildings, along with some other property.

As the fire burned and smoke filled the air, the men did what they could as a crowd of spectators gathered. Emily stood there, shouting words of encouragement to the weary, smudged firemen as the blaze fiercely raged. The fire chief saw the walls begin to waver and called to the crowd for volunteers to help the firemen, but no one stepped forward. The men inside the building were blinded by smoke and needed help to get out alive, but after a second call, no one answered. Emily couldn't take it anymore, and she threw the skirts of her dress over her head and rushed into the burning building. Spectators were shocked and in awe as they waited to see if she would return alive. After a few seconds, she emerged from the smoke, dragging a half-suffocated fireman. They watched as she did this three more times, until all the men were out. She collapsed in the doorway next to the last unconscious fireman she saved from a horrible death.

Onlookers rushed to help her and carried her badly burned body to safety. This striking beauty had sustained horrible burns on her face and hands. She lay unconscious, her once long hair replaced with a scorched and blistered scalp. When Emily regained consciousness, she ignored her own pain and leapt to her feet and began organizing people to help the injured firemen. She tore strips of her own tattered clothing to make bandages for them. She then ordered the men be taken to her nearby house where she knew they would get every comfort and attention to make them well again. Fire Chief David Scannell later recalled, "From that day, she was known as the 'Fire Queen' and became the idol of the fire boys and all who knew her. It was many weeks before she recovered from the effects of her injuries, and to her dying day she bore the honorable scars received on that memorable occasion."[196, 197]

A year later, in August 1856, Mrs. Emily Edwards boarded the clipper *General Wool* and sailed to Melbourne, Australia, to see her husband, where he was running a merchant shop with his father, Hugh, Sr.[198] She stayed briefly and returned to San Francisco that same year. It's not known what happened between them, but she never re-married and reportedly loved him until she died.

Then in 1858, Emily was viciously attacked. A former Massachusetts convict named Coffee and a former California prisoner named Bagley were the perpetrators. By this time, she was calling her Folsom Street brothel the Half-Way House. It was here where Coffee and Bagley forced her out of her house and into the street. They were abusing her when a local laundryman named Henry Gauchet happened upon the scene. He objected to their behavior because of the brutal treatment of a woman. When he did this, they left Emily alone and pulled Gauchet down from his horse. They hit him in the head with a sling-shot, beat him insensible, and then robbed him of all the money he was carrying, which was only about $4 or $5. For good measure, they tossed him over a fence into a pigpen. The two headed for town, but were pursued by a neighbor who had heard the commotion. He led Constable G. W. Glidden to Montgomery Street where the men were. They were so violent that they had to be knocked down to be arrested. Gauchet, although seriously injured, was expected to recover.[199]

Emily's husband Hugh died sometime between March and July 1861 in Australia, and she traveled there to be at his funeral. Upon her return, however, she discovered that her house had been sold to a man named Walter Ringgold. Apparently, Hugh Casement had mort-gaged the property to Henry W. Jones, who had taken possession of the house in Emily's absence and sold it to Ringgold. But Ringgold hadn't yet taken possession of the house, so Emily continued to live there while she and Ringgold spent years in court fighting over who owned the house. Finally, in 1867, a judge ruled in her favor, claim-ing that her husband did not provide any other residence for her, so therefore he must have intended for her to keep it.[200]

In May 1871, a rumor circulated claiming that Emily was seek-ing asylum from her sordid life at the California Rescue Mission. She took out an ad in the *Chronicle* to set the record straight. She stated that her only connection to the Mission was that of helping fallen women who wanted to be redeemed. Emily said she even helped de-fray the costs of these women with her own funds. She also asked the *Chronicle* to print a corrected version of the story, but the paper made it sound like she was receiving money for her charity. Her ad concluded with, "No comment is needed on a newspaper which will refuse to correct where it has made a gross misstatement, without excuse or provocation. Emily Edwards alias the Fire Queen."[201] She eventually moved out of her little house with the fence and oak tree, and by 1874 Emily had rented a house from a former madam named Clara McElroy.[202] By 1880, the fifty-eight-year-old Fire Queen was living in Auburn Township and was the mistress of a house of ill fame. She had two California girls working for her. One was twenty-year-old Amanda Donahue and the other was twenty-four-year-old Mary Tessing.

Emily's paradoxical life came to an end in Colfax on July 15, 1885, and she left a generous will. During her days as a madam, she had acquired a tidy sum and she bequeathed it all to various charities in California and Virginia. The *Placer Argus* listed her charities and amounts she bequeathed, editorializing:

> Although the old woman was among the vilest of the vile, morally speaking, having been the keeper of a house of prostitution for many years, yet—what a strange compound in human nature! She was a woman of good heart in many ways. . . . She was also ready and open-handed when it came to the question of helping the needy if an opportunity were presented. The old woman seems to have been possessed of considerable means for we see by her will, now filed for probate, that she made the following bequests: At San Francisco, Old Ladies' Home, $1,000; Widows' and Orphans' Asylum, $500; Catholic Orphans' Asylum, $500; Society for Benefit of Widows and Orphans of the Police of San Francisco, $500; Sailors' Home, $500; Hospital for Sick Women, $100; Detective John Coffey, $500; James A. Wilson, $500; Margaret Thielacker, $500; David Wolf, $500; Colored M. E. Church of San Francisco, furniture and $250. At Colfax: William Treasure, Sr., $500; August Treasure, $250; Lillie Treasure, $250; Henry Wales, $500; James Wales, $250; Frank Kuenzley, $250; Asa Plank, $250, John L. Butler, gold chain and $250; Ellen Lord, John Lord and Daniel Lord, $250 each.

At Auburn: Richard Rapler, $500; Lotie Huntley, $250; Lincoln Hollenbeck, gold watch and $200; Dr. T. M. Todd, her body to examine and dispose of as he may see proper and $250. Mayor of Richmond, VA, for benefit of colored schools of Richmond, $1,000. Amanda Donahue of Penryn, house and lot in Colfax.[203]

In the end, she had taken care of Amanda Donahue, one of her last prostitutes.

Various Names for the Women and Houses of Prostitution

WOMEN

Chippie

Denizen

Doxy

Inmate

Nefarious

Notorious

Nymph

Nymph du pave

Soiled dove

Sporting girl

Wagtail

Woman of easy virtue

HOUSES

Assignation

Bagnio

Bawdy

Bordello

Brothel

Fancy

House of ill repute or ill fame

Parlor house

6

San Diego

By 1881, San Diego residents were frustrated with the "den of infamy" in the Stingaree district, which they referred to as the "second edition of the Barbary Coast." The locals called their red-light district Stingaree during the 1880s to the early 1900s. Stingaree was located in the lower part of the city where one could find Chinese gambling rooms along J Street between 2nd and 3rd Streets, opium dens, and low houses along G Street and west of 4th. The names of the streets are spelled or designated as they were during the time of the story. At some point some of the numbered streets changed from "street" to "avenue." Chinese and Anglo women worked and lived out of one-story, two-room row houses.

The buildings themselves were owned by prominent local businessmen who leased them out. The townspeople called for the removal of the residents of that area and cited abuse of penal code section 947. The law stated that every person, except a "California Indian," who could physically work and did not for ten days or longer, any healthy person who begged, anyone who associated with thieves or lived in a barn, shop, or house of ill fame, and any prostitute or drunkard should be locked up for ninety days. They concluded that the city was growing, but the negative influence of these people could be detrimental to the new arrivals coming in on daily steamships.[204]

One madam decided to leave Stingaree before things got hot, but she didn't go without leaving a wake of deception. Belle Ashim visited several of San Diego's merchants where she bought a large amount of goods on credit. She then promptly boarded a steamer with her ill-gotten gains and disappeared. The paper wrote, "Now who will sing, 'Empty is the Cradle' with *Chawles* Hawkins?"[205] Charles Hawkins was a local vagrant and a frequent "guest" in the local jail, and "Empty is the Cradle" was a popular song of the time. This was the newspaper's wry way of saying that, with Belle gone, Charles's time in jail would be lonesome.

Six years later, the Stinagaree was running wide open and a Parisian madam named Louise Durant established her brothel there, along with a woman named Ruby, in October 1887. It didn't take long for the law to introduce both of them to the local court. Louise and Ruby were arrested on October 13 for keeping a minor named Lulu Gassel in a house of ill fame. Lulu was also arrested for being a prostitute, and it was believed that Lulu had arrived from Paris only the previous week.[206] It was later learned, however, that Lulu's mother and father swore before Justice Jones that Lulu was over eighteen. Her parents swore that "she was old enough, fat enough, and ugly enough to attend to her own affairs." Louise and Ruby were released and the charges were dismissed.[207]

A year later, city attorney Harry L. Titus was leading the crusade to clean up Stingaree. He wrote of the women who operated there: "The females who inhabit these dens in Stingaree town are the lowest of the low. Disease and filth upon all sides of them. The very air is odorous with debauchery and crime. The women are wrecks of humanity. Blear-eyed, toothless, sallow-faced, and hideous under the use of cheap paint and powder they sit in doorways, dressed in gaudy attire, bedecked with brass jewelry, and coax or invite the passerby to come in."[208] Titus also claimed that when these lewd women weren't trying to attract customers, they drank foul whiskey and sang coarse songs. The women in Stingaree usually had a man called a knocker or fighter to either take care of unruly customers or rob drunkards of their valuables. Titus warned that if Stingaree town wasn't cleaned up soon, he would place signs at every corner entering this area that read, "Hell's Half Acre," which was a popular term of the time for areas like this.[209]

On April 3, 1887, the *San Diego Union* published a large story about vice in the city. The reporter first visited fortune tellers, and then made his way to the brothels, opium dens, and gambling halls. He counted some thirty-five houses of ill fame and more than 120 women, and countless others on the side, "plying their nefarious traffic." He also noted that while the police were making progress in trying to thwart vice, they arrested the offenders only for selling liquor without a license, regardless of their real business. His report cited, "Of these[,] nine cases among keepers of bawdy houses—Madam Georgie, of 4th Street, Madam Ruby, an innocent fourteen-year-old child-appearing offender of 3rd Street, Madam Lizzie, Ruby's neighbor, Ida Bailey of the notorious Sherman House, Madam Louise, a gigantic Scandinavian, near the Sherman House, at whose place the girls were recently arrested for robbing a French waiter of the St. James of $175, Hazel and Edna Russell with six girls, on 6th Street, Madam Stewart, in her elegant 7th Street mansion with name in brazen letters over the door, and a half-dozen girls behind the door; Mrs. Edna G. Barstow, of the disreputable 'Telephone Coffee House,' and last but not least, the leading character of the sketch, that old Madam Cora." Hattie Ruth was also caught up in the fury of arrests and was fined $100 for selling liquor without a license in her brothel at 1309 I Street between 4th and 5th in March and again in December 1887. She quickly paid her fine and went back to business.[210, 211]

A year later, there were over 100 houses of ill fame that contained some 350 inmates. The following madams and their girls thrived in San Diego even while the city was trying to control vice within its jurisdiction.

EDNA RUSSELL

Edna was a 6th Street madam who was detested by most of the good citizens of San Diego. Her business partners were Hazel Russell and Teddy McCarron or Teddy Ann McCann. By the spring of 1887, Edna was running a brothel and had been arrested for selling liquor without a license. This was a common indictment of the time in her fair city, and she fell prey to it again in the summer of 1887 when she was arrested at least twice. She was convicted on the first charge from June 27 for selling liquor without a license at her brothel and was fined $50.[212] A day or two later, she and her six courtesans, one named Bertie Lawrence, were arrested. Edna was booked for luring and keeping underage girls in her notorious house of ill fame, and the girls were hauled in for living there. When police conducted the raid on Edna's house, they found a fourteen-year-old girl named Gretchen Eisel. Gretchen and another young San Francisco girl named Floyd Hasbrook had first met Edna Russell when they boarded a steamer from San Francisco to San Diego. Apparently, Edna promised the girls positions in her house and they accepted. After the raid, police asked the girls about their family situations. Gretchen said that her father worked as an ivory turner and treated her cruelly, but Floyd refused to tell officials who her father was or what he did for a living.[213]

It was later revealed that Gretchen was not the innocent child officers first believed her to be. Upon further investigation, and according to Gretchen herself, she was a willing participant and resident of Edna's establishment. She professed to reveling in the fast life, and Edna's place was not her first foray into the business. In fact, she had been a girl of easy virtue for quite some time. Deputy Constable Tucker tried to persuade Gretchen to stay with him and his wife so she wouldn't have to go to jail. But Gretchen glibly refused and said she would rather go to jail with the other girls and see what it was all about. The district attorney was perplexed at what to do with this minor since she clearly was not going to abandon her ways. The citizenry hoped he would secure her a home in an orphan asylum until she could realize the errors of her ways. Meanwhile, all six courtesans remained in jail with their bail set at $500. A week later, Gretchen was sent to a Los Angeles home for fallen women. Edna and Teddy's court date was set for early July, with their bail at $300 each. The district attorney was determined to shut down brothels in his city. He wanted to prohibit this "species" of woman from flaunting their expensive clothes as they paraded or rode in open carriages on the city streets.[214]

On July 9, 1887, the courtroom was filled with bald-headed men, young boys, and many more spectators eager to get a glimpse of the fallen women. In the end, there wasn't enough evidence against Edna, four of her courtesans, or Teddy McCarron. There was, however, a charge and countercharge of battery between Bertie Lawrence and Teddy.[215] Two months later, Edna swallowed twenty-one grains of morphine and consumed a large amount of opium. Rescuers thwarted her suicide attempt, but soon after, she disappeared from history.[216]

SARAH KATHERINE EVANS, AKA KATE CLARK

She was born Sarah Katherine "Kate" Evans, but history remembers her as Kate Clark. It was between 1876 and 1878 when she took that name, and by 1884, she was living in Prescott, Arizona. While there she married Patrick Bradley on December 9, 1884. By July 1886, she had settled in San Diego at 335 6th, and that month she applied for a liquor license but was denied. That didn't stop Kate, and soon she and her business partner, Annie Ellis, were running a gaudily decorated double house-bagnio on 6th Street.

In May 1887, Kate traveled from San Diego north to San Rafael in the Bay Area. There, the owners of the Delmonico Restaurant, Louis T. Pigot and Charles Vanemon, were opening a new mine. As part of a celebration at the start of newly installed machinery, they asked Kate to blow the first whistle. The local citizens of San Diego did not object to her absence. While in San Rafael, she assumed the name of Mrs. Pigot, suggesting that she and Louis Pigot were likely more than just friends.[217]

Kate's most notorious story begins with a fourteen-year-old blonde girl who was brothel hopping in San Francisco as she looked for a job. This teenager was a woman in every sense of the word and appeared to be at least eighteen. She stood a half-head taller than other girls her age, was slender, and "well-matured." In mid-August 1887, her alleged procurer, Dennis McCarthy, was arrested in San Francisco for enticing a young girl named Julia Seiler into madam Inez Leonard's brothel on Ellis Street. During McCarthy's subsequent court appearance, several different versions of events came to light.

Inez recalled that, on Sunday, July 31, she was sitting in her parlor playing cards when the doorbell rang. She waited before answering and nothing happened, so she went back to her game. About ten minutes later it rang again. The houseboy who worked for her announced there was a young man and girl wishing to see her. Inez told him to show them upstairs where she soon joined them. Inez realized this was the girl McCarthy had written to her about. She asked Julia, "Don't you think you are a foolish girl, wanting to leave your home?" Julia agreed, but asked to stay and use one of Inez's rooms so she and McCarthy could be intimate together under a brothel roof. Inez agreed and let her stay until the next night so she could leave under the cover of darkness. But before Julia left, Inez received a visit from one of her former girls named Nellie Leslie, who now worked for Kate Clark. Julia left Inez's around 8 P.M. that night,[218] but Nellie took her to Kate's place. Inez was later arrested and "the little girl returned to her home" at 202 Ellis Street.[219]

Julia told a different story. She said she knew at an early age what she wanted to do and professed she was a girl who did not want to change her wayward habits. Despite desperate pleas from her mother and father, she left home at the beginning of August and sought out madams who would hire her. She heard that Kate Clark was in town and looked her up after Inez turned her down. When Kate inquired about her age, Julia lied and said she was eighteen. Kate doubted Julia, so she told her she had all the girls she needed. Julia persisted and was provoked by Kate's comments because her heart was set on living a fast life. But Kate stood firm.

With the determination of a miner on the hunt for treasure, Julia disguised herself by dyeing her hair brown and then boarded the same boat Kate and her partner Annie Ellis were returning to San Diego aboard. The *Santa Rosa* set sail for San Diego, and on the second day of the journey, as Kate strolled the deck, Julia approached her again.

The disguised Julia told Kate she had no money and needed to get away from her mean father. Kate said she would gladly help, and since Julia's hair was disheveled from being on deck, Kate took her to her stateroom and combed and braided it for her. Kate remarked how beautiful the girl's hair was, and Julia told Kate that she was of Indian descent. Kate had not discovered Julia's secret, but her companion Nellie Leslie had. She said to Kate, "Don't you know that girl? It's the same one that ran away and had her hair dyed in the city." Kate told Nellie she was mistaken and she didn't see the resemblance.[220] Kate finally learned of Julia's deception, and the girl was devastated that her plan had failed. Julia also learned that friends of her father were in San Diego, so in a last effort, she feigned an illness and again begged Kate to take her, which she did.[221]

On August 23, Kate received a special letter that was delivered by Isador Louis, who was a friend of Julia's father. In it, he told Kate that Julia's father, David Seiler, a clothing merchant on Market Street, was willing to make sure that she didn't face any troubles if she agreed to pay Isador $150 for legal and Julia's travel expenses back home. Kate said, "As I wished to avoid any trouble, I paid the money, and here is the receipt."[222] On August 25, Kate was hauled back to San Francisco to stand trial on a charge of enticing Julia into her San Diego brothel.

While Kate awaited her trial, Dennis McCarthy's case finally came to trial in December 1887. When she testified, Julia blamed McCarthy for introducing her into a life of shame. She later testified that she begged Dennis to take her to Inez's place. The newspaper stated she was no ordinary girl and carried herself with an air of experience and confidence. They were not convinced that anyone could entice her into doing something she didn't want. Dennis testified that Julia sent letters to him daily begging him to get her into Inez's brothel. He said that she wanted the Parisian dresses and the luxurious life she believed these women had. According to Dennis, he agreed to do as Julia wished, but only after speaking with Inez, who said she would try to convince Julia to not start in the business. When they arrived at Inez's, Julia refused to talk and insisted on sharing a room with Dennis, which they did. Julia was worried that her night of shame would get back to her parents, so she had Dennis take her to San Diego. They told Kate the story of an abusive father because Julia didn't want to return to San Francisco. The jury was deadlocked and the charges against Kate were dismissed.[223]

A second trial for Kate's association with Julia Seiler took place in the spring of 1888 during which one of Kate's courtesans, Nellie Leslie, testified. During the entire testimony, Julia beamed with smiles and giggled often. Nellie stated that she and Kate took the steamship *Santa Rosa* in the spring of 1887 from San Francisco to San Diego where they met a girl named Julia Seiler. Julia told them she was eighteen and was anxious to leave home and begin a life of shame. She also told Kate that her father had shut her out of their house and she had run away. Kate felt sorry for her and agreed to let the girl live with her for a couple of days because she was penniless. On her second day at Kate's house, Julia told her she was only fourteen and Kate promptly took her to the police station. Kate was soon arrested for enticing a young girl into her brothel and Julia was taken back to San Francisco.[224] Nellie's testimony corroborated what Julia had stated back in August.

Kate fled and in July 1888 was living in Los Angeles where she used her maiden name of Evans, going by Mrs. Kate Evans. It was reported that she was "sojourning" in the city with her beau, one Louis Pigot, who owned a French restaurant in the city. Local law officers learned of her presence and went to interview her, but found only Mr. Pigot and what the papers called "her little girl." Pigot finally confessed that Kate had gone to Colton, so they telegraphed Marshal Virgil Earp to look for her. The next day Earp replied that he had Kate in his custody.

Deputy Manning headed to Colton and escorted Kate back to San Francisco. Once there, she somehow escaped. A judge issued a bench warrant, but on July 6, recalled the warrant in lieu of a $1,000 bond, which was deposited.[225] The next day, Kate took to the newspapers and blasted the police for trying to extort money from her, saying that the Seiler case was nothing more than a blackmailing scheme. She and her lawyer pledged to sue the city of San Francisco for false arrests and other charges. To further her cause, she stated that if officials didn't leave her alone, she would share certain information that would shock all. She also said that she had been reformed, sold her brothel, and would never set foot in a house of ill fame even if she had to take in clothes and do washing.[226] The next day, she was arrested in Los Angeles but was later freed on her own recognizance.

Another trial ensued and on August 10, 1888, at 10 A.M., she and her attorney arose in the courtroom to hear the verdict. It had been over a year since Kate has been accused of abducting Julia Seiler. She was found not guilty.[227]

Kate went back to her business, as evidenced by a liquor license issued in March 1892, and that's the last known detail of her life.

BELLE WENTWORTH

Belle Wentworth was a 3rd Street courtesan with a lover named A. J. Perkins. In the spring of 1887, she and Perkins were arrested for robbing a black-mustached Frenchman of $175 and his purse. When they made their appearance in court, District Attorney Copeland was stunned to find a large crowd of onlookers. He immediately called for the courtroom to be cleared and the ponderous doors closed. He began his oration with:

> This feast of nastiness, of which the people of this city have been partaking in this Court for the last few weeks during the trials of these women, is deteriorating their morals, is cultivating their taste for things low and vile and is overcoming the consciences of even the most upright. It is a sad spectacle to see these hungerings and thirstings after things forbidden, and the officers of the law, whose business it is to conserve public morals, ought to not pander to these desires.

During the trial, it was determined that there was no evidence to arrest Wentworth and Perkins for theft, so they were freed. Then they were both immediately arrested again—Belle for keeping a house of ill fame and Perkins for being an opium smoker and vagrant.[228] It's possible this arrest caused her to leave town because she was not heard from again.

Ida Bailey, aka Annie McLendon or "Red-Headed Ida"

Ida Bailey is remembered as one of San Diego's most notorious madams, yet her story remains hazy, as many madams' histories are, because such large pieces of it are missing from the record. What is known, by all documented evidence, is that she was born in Canada in February 1872 as Annie L. M. Barth. Her father was John A. B. Barth from Scotland and her mother was Annie O'Connell from Canada. It appears they immigrated to the United States in either 1875 or 1879, and Annie was possibly married for the first time in 1890.

A woman named Ida Bailey entered the demimonde world as a prostitute for the notorious madam Catherine Reiter in San Francisco around 1883, but it's uncertain whether she was *this* Ida Bailey. This was the same Catherine Reiter who fought in court to keep the Victorian fashion ensembles that she provided to that Ida. The San Francisco Ida Bailey disappeared from that city and this one appeared here in 1889. If, in fact, this was the same Ida Bailey, then she would have been only eleven years old when she worked for Catherine. It wasn't uncommon for girls to be prostitutes that young, but wouldn't the judge who handled her case against Reiter have noticed and said something? If it is the same Ida, then that would make her about thirteen when she arrived in San Diego, and while that's still young, it wouldn't have been unusual in that era.

By 1885, an Ida Bailey appeared in San Diego and started her own business. It was called the Sherman House and was nestled among first-class residential homes on 3rd and I Streets. (San Diego used numerals for numbered street names; later, these streets were changed to avenues.) In July the following year, her application for a wholesale liquor license was granted. Things were going just fine for Ida until she was fined for not having a liquor license. She claimed she had paid to renew her license and put up a $100 bond while awaiting a decision. That same year, the city attorney formed a special committee to visit disreputable houses, which included Ida's. They reported that Ida told them she had paid both her county license fee and her U.S. revenue tax.[229] By 1889, Ida was living at 253 6th with Ollie Baker, Rosie

Bradley, Lita Garde, Iva Stanley, and Mrs. W. E. Castle, who stated she was an "inmate" of Ida Bailey's.[230]

City officials and citizens alike were increasingly fed up with the vice in San Diego, and Ida was a popular target. In July 1891, she was arrested for selling liquor without a license. A hearing was held two months later. Ida asked for a jury trial, which was denied, much to the delight of city police. Ida's attorney then asked for a change of venue because he felt the court was a material witness and she wouldn't get a fair trial. That, too, was denied. In the end, Ida was found guilty and told to pay a $50 fine or spend twenty-five days in jail. She promptly paid the fine.[231]

Leap ahead to January 1899 and we see that her landlord, John Kastle, tried to eject her from the house.[232] He tried again in March, but she refused to leave. He asked the court to award him $70, which amounted to the two months' rent she owed him.[233] Ida knew her eviction was inevitable, so she moved out and relocated to 251 5th, where she ran the Golden West lodgings. Kastle dropped the case.[234] Her "lodgings house" included ten residents, including six other women: Mrs. W. A. Gould, Eva Finning, Annie and Agnes Bith, Freida Meyer, and Mrs. Helen Ordway. Three male tenants included laborers John Lee and Joe Chandler, along with Norwood Ellwood, who worked as a porter at a bar.[235]

Within two months at her new location, Ida's red-headed temper got the town's attention. At about 11 P.M. on June 17, a jealous Ida slapped the buxom Mrs. Kate—"Coffee Kate"—Grigsby while they were standing at the corner of 4th and D Streets. Kate was said to be the third wife of Sergeant Grisby, who was being charged with bigamy. Before the police arrived, Ida escaped in a hack and rode away. Just why Ida was jealous of Coffee Kate is unknown, but the incident happened right around the time Kate found out she was wife number three.[236]

Ida had an affection for children, and she was heartbroken when she lost one of her own. Afterward, she began to adopt and care for orphans and donate to local charities. When young Augustine and George Lambla's father murdered their mother and then shot himself, she cared for them. Augustine moved out, but George stayed, even though he was a twelve-year-old living in a brothel. His companions were prostitutes Virna Zelleker, Dora Henning, and Mamie Beck.

By the fall of 1901, Ida was still operating her brothel, but had moved yet again, and this time landed on lower 4th Avenue. On the evening of October 1, a carriage drove by her establishment and an occupant fired a shot into her open front door. No one was injured, but the bullet missed Ida by a foot. No one was ever charged in the incident.[237]

It wasn't uncommon for johns to fall in love with their prostitutes and want to take them away. In March 1902, one of Ida's girls, Madeline Grinder, fell in love with Private John Commer of the 11th Company. He was stationed at the guardhouse and proudly wore his uniform when the pair were married. They didn't exactly have a typical wedding night. Madeline went back to Ida's, and John returned to the barracks and bragged about his wedding. He was promptly charged with disgracing his uniform.[238]

By this time, the area where the brothels were located was called the Tenderloin or the Stingaree district, as riddled with vice as San Francisco's notorious Barbary Coast. Not surprisingly, trouble seemed to follow Ida, and in April 1902, she and two of her competitors, Ida Gould and Mamie Goldstein, were arraigned for selling liquor without a license. This Ida Gould disappeared shortly after her arrest. When Ida Bailey appeared before the judge, she quickly and quietly entered a not guilty plea and posted a $100 bond. She was released until the hearing.[239] Two weeks later, the case was dismissed for insufficient evidence.[240]

By 1903, Ida was residing at 530 4th, in what the locals called the "canary cottage," due to its pale-yellow color. Even though the locals called it that, Ida never used that name in the local business directories. The house was a tidy little story-and-a-half cottage with white trim that sat behind a white picket fence, with two big magnolia trees out in the front yard.[241] Ida liked to advertise her girls and flaunt her business, so on pleasant Sunday afternoons, she would send for a barouche from the Diamond Carriage Company. She liked barouches, because the top could be let down and she could show off four of her best-looking girls, dressed up in their finest clothes. They paraded through the residential districts, which eventually led to a crack-down.[242] San Diego's female residents were tired of women like Ida and Mamie Goldstein being allowed to keep their parlor houses. That's when Mrs. J. Cherry and Mrs. Watkins of the Social Purity League swore out complaints. In a late-night raid in the summer of 1904, the police arrested Ida and her girls. They also arrested Goldstein and her girls. This time, however, instead of booking them for selling liquor without a license, they were charged with keeping houses of ill fame. In addition to Ida and Mamie, the police also arrested Jane Doe, Susie Doe, Sarah Doe, Beatrice Hill/Heald, and Marguerite Smith, all for vagrancy. The madams each gave $100 bonds and the girls furnished $20 cash bail each.[243] Both madams pleaded not guilty. A month later, the prosecution was ready to begin the trial, but they were having a hard time filling the jury box. The attorneys went through 120 potential jurors and finally filled out the jury on August 2. While this was going on, an embezzler by the name of Harry Leonard, alias Alfred Gage, was arrested in Ida's parlor house. Ida's trial began on August 3 and quickly ended in a nine to three vote in favor of acquittal. The district attorney immediately announced he would try her again with stronger evidence.[244]

This time, the complaint was sworn out against Ida by the police department and not the Social Purity League, which had withdrawn its original complaint. Ida was rearrested, and she posted another bond until her trial, which was set for September 1. Once again, the prosecution had a hard time finding jurors for the trial. It took them ten days to complete the jury. The case was postponed and eventually dismissed in late September when Ida changed her plea to guilty and paid a fine.[245]

Between 1904 and 1905, Ida moved from her parlor house at 530 4th to a boarding house at 548 12th. Around this time, she met her one true love, and it appears that she quit playing the role of madam.

William Boyd McLendon was born in Marlborough, South Carolina, in November 1872. He had been a farmer, then later served in the U.S. Army. William was in San Diego after he had been honorably discharged in 1898, but then he reenlisted. It's not known why, but in 1904, William was sent to military prison, and in June, he was dishonorably discharged. Just how and when he met Ida is a mystery, but Ida fell in love and soon married the blue-eyed, six-foot Southerner on October 17, 1905, in St. Joseph's Church. Father Antonio Ubach performed the ceremony and entered Ida's name as Miss Annie L. M. Barth in the church's marriage register.[246] Her adopted son, George Lambla, was one of the witnesses. Annie then moved into William's house at 1114 G Street, where she was known as Annie McLendon, wife of William. Even though she was now Mrs. Annie McLendon, the papers continued to refer to her as Ida—sometimes Bailey and other times McLendon.

In 1907, Ida and William took in a young girl named Lucille. The girl's mother, a red-light district resident named Fay Harmon, asked Ida to take care of Lucille because her paramour, Billy Douglas, had assaulted the little girl. But then Fay changed her mind. She swore out a writ of habeas corpus to remove her five-year-old daughter from Ida's home. When both Ida and Chief of Police Thomas resisted Fay's efforts to regain custody of Lucille, she pressed charges against them.[247] Fay was later charged with vagrancy. Fortunately for Lucille, the little girl's grandmother, who lived in San Pedro, said she was fit to care for the child and wanted custody.[248] The grandmother was given custody, and Lucille went to live with her.

In early May 1907, Ida was running a boarding house and William worked at the local lumber mill. William had developed heart trouble and for several months complained of it. He threatened to end his own life on many occasions, but the last time Ida caught him. Just as he was ready to slit his throat, she stopped him. He told her, "I am going to kill myself. I am tired of life." A few days after that incident he came home from his job at the local lumber mill and said to Ida, "My heart is weak; give me some bromidia." She gave him a two-ounce bottle of this popular elixir of the time, a mixture of "Hydrate of chloral, Bromide of potassium, Hyoscyamus, and Cannabis-Indica," with an alcohol content of ten percent. William took just a small sip.

Later that day he went to the barbershop and when he came home, he asked Ida to make him some dinner. She went into the kitchen while William drank the rest of the bromide. When she came back, she found him lifeless. She woke the residents in her boarding house and sent them for help. Doctors tried to revive William for two hours, but the thirty-five-year-old died on May 7. Ida believed that William purchased something when he went out and added it to the bromide when she wasn't looking.[249] She buried him in Mount Hope Cemetery.

While William was alive, she went by the name Annie, but in the obituary and burial records she gave her name as Ida.[250] After William died, Ida created a hybrid of names and often mixed Ida and Annie, and Bailey and McLendon. The papers frequently referred to her as "Annie McLendon also known as Ida Bailey." Ida listed herself as the widow of William McLendon in the local business directory for the rest of her life.

After William died, Ida began calling her rooming house "The Marion."[251] William had been born and raised in Marion County, South Carolina. The 1910 U.S. Census taken in April indicates that Annie McLendon was running a legitimate boarding house with two men as boarders. By then, she had given birth to three children, but none of them lived. She did have a six-year-old godson named Ivoal Marze living with her. Despite the appearance of a legitimate house, an October arrest report offers another version. Ida was arrested for keeping a disorderly house outside of the red-light district on G Street between 2nd and 3rd. Unfortunately, her establishment was just around the corner from the police station, and she and two occupants, Jane Doe (aka Rickey Bowman) and Virginia Martin or Morton, were arrested for vagrancy and charged with leading a lewd and dissolute life. Jane Doe forfeited $25 and Virginia spent twenty-four hours in jail.[252]

Ida continued to live at the house where she and William lived until 1914 when she moved to 214 G Street where she offered lodgings. The 1920 U.S. Census shows Annie McLendon running a lodging house. She listed two children living with her, Beatrice and Robert Roy Edmons, as well as her godson, Ivoal Marze/Marcus. The Edmons children's mother lived with Ida in 1912 and 1913. Her boarders then included a father, Roy Staggs, and his two children, and four laborers.

In the spring of 1921, Ida had some strange guests living at 214 G Street: a family cat named Malty and a rescued pigeon named Major Hufeland. This animal menagerie piqued the curiosity of the *San Diego*

Union, which sent a reporter to investigate. The reporter learned that about two months prior, one of the tenants had found the bird covered in crude oil. It was apparent the bird was a pet because its wings were clipped. When the boarder could not find the pigeon's owner, he brought it home to Robert Edmons. Major Hufeland was allowed to wander around the entire house and lived among the people as he pleased. In April, Malty gave birth to kittens and Ida provided them with a crate for safety. Major Hufeland became very protective of the five kittens and as soon as Malty left for any reason, the pigeon would jump down on the crate and hover over the kittens. If anyone picked up a kitten, Major Hufeland pecked and scratched until the kitten was replaced. Neither Ida nor Robert could explain the odd connection between the pigeon and the cats.[253]

In September 1922, Ida almost lost everything to a fire. Fortunately for her, the fire department reacted quickly, and her property suffered only minor damage. She did, however, lose a large quantity of expensive clothing in the blaze.[254]

Nearly sixty years later, local resident Jerry MacMullen remembered seeing Ida when he was a young man. He recalled:

Well, I saw her in about 1922, just after I had gone to work as a police reporter on the *Tribune*. This pathetic-looking old woman used to come shuffling by the police station occasionally—that's when they had that horrible old police station down on Second Street, between F and G—and she would stop for a moment and chat with some of the old-timers like [police sergeant] George Pringle, [patrolman] George Wilson, or [patrolman] Jack Golden. One day, after she had gone on shuffling down the street, I asked George Pringle, 'Who is that dreadful-looking old bag?' He said, 'Why, don't you know, that is Ida Bailey!' She was still living and much the worse for the wear. But you could tell she had been a 'humdinger' in her day. So, I was very proud of the fact that I had seen Ida Bailey.[255]

In 1922, Ida would have been only fifty years old.

After the fire, Ida stayed out of trouble until February 1923 when

Annie McLendon aka Ida Bailey was arrested for selling moonshine from her house to Roy Staggs. Staggs was an electrician and long-time tenant of Ida's. They were both arrested when she sold him a half-pint flask of a very poor grade "whiskey" for $2. He was promptly arrested for disturbing the peace. Federal Prohibition officer Charles Cass arrested Ida, and when he searched her house, he found twenty pints of the same liquor. She had it stashed in a suitcase. They took Ida and her spirits to the police station around the corner where she was booked and charged with violating the Volstead Act. Her bail was set at $2,000.[256] Two months later, she and Staggs were arrested by detectives Rochfort and Newsom for violating California's Wright Act (which enacted federally mandated Prohibition at the state level) for having a gallon of "white mule" in her home. She pleaded guilty and paid a $150 fine in U.S. district court. The court reduced her fine to $50 when they learned that she adopted and raised orphans and made generous donations to local charities.[257]

Her longtime tenant Staggs soon married a woman named Eva and moved to Maywood, California. It was there where his wife murdered him. The papers reported he was a pleasant man when sober, but when drunk became violent. He frequently beat his wife and on one occasion used a chair. Witnesses said she did everything she could to get away from him, but he was relentless. She shot him and the police ruled the killing was justified.[258] One has to wonder if he became violent with Ida despite getting his illegal liquor from her.

The last verifiable address for Ida Annie Bailey McLendon was 141 F in 1926.[259] By the time the 1930 U.S. census was taken, Ida was not counted. Beatrice and Robert Edmons were living in an orphanage called the Nazareth House. The details of Ida's death are unknown, but it's reasonable to assume that she died sometime between 1926 and 1930.

7

San Jose and Santa Clara County

Santa Clara County sits just south of San Francisco in a well-protected valley that native peoples, missionaries, and pioneers all found inviting in their time. Other towns in the county include Gilroy, Los Gatos, and San Jose. Founded in 1777, San Jose was California's first civil town (not affiliated with a mission or military post) and later became California's first state capital in 1849. The county was connected by early railroads and boasted fruit orchards, artesian well water, and oil wells. The towns all had brothels and saloons, too!

San Jose had its own version of the Barbary Coast that included houses of ill fame along El Dorado Street (today's Post Street) near Market, Orchard, and Vine Streets. In 1885, nearly seventy-five women were reportedly working in those houses. Locals were infuriated when it appeared some of the town's "so-called" respectable citizens were building such houses and making sure they were well-furnished.

Such was the case of T. J. Gillespie. In March 1885, Eliza Good, owner of the William Tell House at the corner of El Dorado and San Pedro Streets, filed a complaint that Gillespie had rented a house to Lizzie Stone for the purpose of a brothel. Lizzie was taken before Justice Pfister and let free once she agreed to leave the city. Mr. Gillespie was considered a pious man and a good Christian, but he apparently owned several houses where women were running houses of ill fame. Many believed there had to be some kind of mistake.[260] Regardless, Lizzie disappeared rather quickly.

Another vanishing madam was Clara Taylor. When Officer Salisbury discovered that Clara was running a brothel within the city limits, he did his best to put her out of business. During the last three months of 1885, he tried to arrest her more than once. Each time Salisbury tried, however, Clara moved to a new location. She was arrested in October but promptly moved and then was booked again in December 1885 for keeping a house of ill fame on Fourth Street just north of Santa Clara Street. Salisbury must have persisted because no further information can be found on Clara in the record.

In addition to efforts like those of Officer Salisbury, San Jose's citizens walked door to door on a crusade to end prostitution. They collected signatures, and in 1886 they presented a petition to the city council to remove the brothels. The mayor responded by saying that every effort had been made to remove them, but he agreed to try again. A previous approach implemented by Chief of Police Dan Haskell had worked well. Haskell had seen to it that brothel entrances were illuminated, and he had stationed an officer at each house to write down the names of every person who went in or out. Once word had gotten out that "secret" visits to houses were going to be made public, traffic dried up and the houses closed. The new petition suggested the council try that method again.[261]

In 1887, the San Jose *Evening News* posed a good question to its readers when it asked why only the women who operated and worked in the brothels were arrested. The paper suggested that if the men who patronized these places were also fined, then business would slow and the brothels would eventually go away. The editors wrote, "If the fine is punishment for an offense against publics morals . . .

the men have offended equally, if not more, than the women, and certainly should be punished with an equal or heavier fine. To punish these fallen women, while their patrons go free, will never restrict the evil or protect society."[262] Apparently, city officials heeded the advice and did a fairly good job of keeping brothels to a minimum— madams didn't last long in their city. Because of this, the following stories are brief.

Mrs. Eva H. Davis

Eva Davis played in two cities and also seems to have started in San Francisco before landing in San Jose. She and her husband, Michael L. King, set up a brothel. They bought furniture and other items to make the house inviting, and by the fall of 1883, her business was up and running. They encountered a minor setback when Martin Bachrach filed a suit against them for failing to pay for the household goods worth $386 and another $100 for damages sustained from withholding the goods.[263] The nature of the suit is confusing because Bachrach wasn't a merchant—he worked at the Baldwin Theatre and Grand Opera House as its chorus master in the late 1870s and early 1880s. Eva may have thought that when Bachrach died in early 1885, his suit against them did too. But she was wrong—Bachrach's administrator, Philip A. Roach, continued to fight for the money Bachrach was owed.

In January 1886, Eva's landlord, Antonio Vatuone, offered her $100 to quietly leave his building. Knowing he wanted her brothel gone and was willing to pay, she demanded $250 instead. He chose not to pay what she demanded and complained to the city. After an unsuccessful attempt to get her to move, the police employed Dan Haskell's technique, and a bright lantern was shone onto the front of her residence. A police officer was also stationed outside to take down all the names of the people who came and went. This tactic didn't work on Eva, so a formal complaint was filed. Around this time, Eva bought a house at 333 San Fernando Street from Samuel Cobb.

After Haskell's plan failed, city officials used Eva's debt to Bachrach as an excuse to put her San Fernando Street house on the block at a sheriff's sale. They waited a month and then acted, claiming that Eva and King still owed Bachrach for the goods they bought, which now totaled $486 plus $65.85 interest. The Superior Court judge ordered the sheriff's sale and the house was put up for auction on June 5, 1886.[264] She then moved into a room in the Winchester Building on First.

Apparently Eva did not lose her house and stayed in San Jose for quite some time. In 1893, she was "asked to visit" Justice King on November 24 to explain why she beat up a person named W. Roubai. In May the following year, Eva was in the middle of negotiating a trade of her properties on San Fernando Street with Francis and Charles Lovett for their boarding house at 254 North First Street. Before the deal was completed, she discovered the Lovetts had failed to tell her there was a $656 lien on their property. Since she faced losing her property, she sued them to recover the money.[265]

By 1895, Eva and her sons were still on North First Street, where she was operating her business called the Harmony Hamman baths. In early 1895, her eldest son, Paul, accused John Doe, a junk dealer, of petty larceny for stealing a rubber shoe, some bottles, and old clothing. Then in mid-May, Harry Lapier, who often visited Eva's baths, took something that didn't belong to him on one of his visits. Sometime after he was gone, Eva noticed that her treasure box with a diamond ring, $15 in coin, and valuable papers were missing. She looked inside the house and then headed for the yard, where she discovered the empty box in a nearby woodpile. Eva wanted justice, so she called Officer Monahan, who came to her house to take her report. They hatched a plan to catch the thief and put the box back in the woodpile. Officer Monahan watched and waited. At about 11 P.M. that night, Lapier returned to retrieve the box and was promptly arrested. Eva refused to press charges, but Justice Gass gave Lapier the option of a $40 fine or thirty days in jail.[266] About ten days later, Eva went to Los Angeles. Some citizens resorted to drastic measures when they wanted the demimonde gone. Fire was one of their tactics, and for a third time in 1896 someone set a fire in the stairway in the hall on the first floor of Eva's house. When she arrived home, she was relieved to see that once again, the damage was minimal.[267] In July, a more serious blaze left one of Eva's girls, Sadie Abbott, nearly asphyxiated by smoke.

Her son had moved to San Diego for a while, but he came back quickly and went to work for his mother as a clerk. Two years later, a woman named Virginia Cereghino filed a foreclosure suit against Eva for the sum of $8,210. The judge ordered that the house on First Street be sold to satisfy the debt. The house fetched $8,733.03.[268] This sale seems to be the end of Eva, and this is where her story fades into obscurity.

MABEL WEST

When Mabel West decided to open her brothel, she struck up a deal with a saloon owner in Gilroy named Tom Fox. By doing this, Tom gained some extra customers, while Mabel's clients could appear as if they were simply entering a saloon.

Mabel was preparing for the 1888 Valentine season at her El Dorado Street brothel when she was arrested. Her problems had begun in November 1887 when she took on a new, pretty brunette named Mary Rhodes. Mary was a fifteen-year-old from Tulare and the daughter of A. R. Rhodes. A few months earlier, Mary had started a regular job at the Los Gatos Fruit Company in Tulare. Her father entrusted her to a family friend named Nellie Rosser. It was a decision that her father soon deeply regretted. Mary drifted around for a while and then made her way, with Nellie's help, to Gilroy where she found Mabel.

So, in February, when Mary's father discovered what his daughter was doing, he raced back to Gilroy. Once there, he accused Mabel of enticing his minor daughter into her place for immoral purposes. She and Fox were both arrested and sat in the county jail until their trial. Judge Pfister's crowded court promptly convened at 10 A.M. on February 11, 1888. Both Mabel and Tom attended, along with their legal counsel, W. G. Lorigan. Unfortunately for Lorigan, his clients were clearly guilty and he could do nothing for them. The district attorney was so outraged over the case that he implored the judge to impose the most severe penalty allowable by law. During the trial, Mr. Rhodes became emotional and could not hold back his tears as he listened to the details. His daughter, on the other hand, was very engaged and watched the proceedings intently.[269]

At the conclusion of the trial, both Mabel and Tom were found guilty. She was sentenced to four months in the county jail for keeping a minor in a house of ill fame, and Fox was sentenced to five months in prison. The young Mary returned to her father's home where it was hoped her brief stint as a working girl would soon be forgotten, especially because of her "repentant manner."

Five months later, in June, the paper noted that Mabel was "at liberty" after having served her sentence. Her trail goes cold with her release from jail.

8

Central Coast

The Central Coast region includes the towns of Ventura, Santa Barbara, Monterey, San Benito, Santa Cruz, and San Luis Obispo. The area was home to several early Spanish missions.

Like many other California towns, Santa Cruz received an influx of empty-pocketed gold rush miners. Originally a Spanish mission town, by the mid-1850s Santa Cruz took on a more Anglican appearance as wooden houses and fences began to replace adobe structures. Lumber camps, limestone quarries, tanneries, and agriculture (including grapes for wine), allowed Santa Cruz to flourish.

While the town was growing in all the right ways, it was also growing in some of the wrong ways. Town officials wanted to make it clear that they would not allow anyone to run a brothel within city limits. They passed Ordinance 57, which forbade the establishment of brothels or renting a building for such purpose. Anyone caught and convicted of violating this ordinance would face a fine of up to $100 and up to thirty days in prison or both.[270]

By 1881, houses of ill fame had also become a significant problem for the town of San Luis Obispo. Its citizens questioned why their local law officers were not enforcing the regulations and further asked why should laws exist if they weren't going to be enforced. Three years later, the townspeople were still not satisfied and the local paper reported, "Many vagrants and inmates of houses of ill fame have made this city a rendezvous for the eking out of a nefarious livelihood long enough. There can be no question about it. This town must be cleared of this class of citizen. San Luis is comparatively but sparsely settled. She has room for thousands of industrious people."[271] Welcome to the madams of the Central Coast.

Maurisia Duarte

Maurisia Duarte's life was complicated, and what she did for a living may come as a surprise to her descendants.

Maurisia was born about 1838 in San Jose del Cabo, Mexico, to Jose and Maria Duarte. She was the youngest of seventeen children. This large family packed up their belongings, and by 1850 they

Maurisia Duarte, center. PHOTOGRAPH COURTESY OF LEONARD TURNBULL.

John José Brown, Maurisia's son. PHOTOGRAPH COURTESY OF LEONARD TURNBULL.

had made their way to Monterey, California. Just two years later, her father died there. It was around 1856 when Maurisia married Englishman William Brown, who worked as a carman on a train. Not long after the union, the couple welcomed a daughter named Tomasa "Tomasita" Mary Brown on March 7, 1857. Two years later, Maurisia gave birth to John José "JJ" Brown on June 19, 1859. According to the 1860 census, the family lived a modest life with personal assets of $500 and real estate holdings valued at $700.

Maurisia lost William sometime between 1860 and 1864, and later married William LaPorte. The couple moved to San Luis Obispo, where they welcomed the new year of 1865 with a daughter named Annie May "Brown" LaPorte. Maurisia's marriage to LaPorte was very brief and they soon separated (he died in 1883). By April 1866, Maurisia had married Juan De Dio Espinosa and gave birth to child number four. Juan and Maurisia welcomed Leonardo S. Espinosa to their Creston Road home in San Luis Obispo. About a year later, the cries of a new infant were heard when Ida "Brown" Espinosa arrived, followed in due time by a baby brother named Jake. Maurisia and Juan were married at least until 1869.

With a brood of children—and possibly widowed once again—Maurisia needed to earn an income, so she turned to what many desperate women did and became a madam. In late 1881, Maurisia Duarte was charged with allowing minors into her house of ill fame, but the judge ruled that there wasn't sufficient evidence to support the charge and she was allowed go free.[272] Yet she had neglected to pay her taxes of $2.76 for the year 1882–1883, so her personal property, fixtures, furniture, a buggy and harness, and one horse were to be sold at auction in February 1883. It's not known what happened, but she was granted a business license to operate a dance house within the city limits from November 1883 until February 1884. The license was revoked in early December for being a detriment to the good morals of the city. The mayor noted that most, if not all, of the crimes committed in his city happened at or near dance houses. He wrote, "Drunkenness and crime, debauchery and depravity appear to run rife in and around said houses."[273] By May, it appears she left town and did not bother to pick up a letter that was waiting for her at the post office.

Maurisia returned to San Luis Obispo (or perhaps had just kept a low profile) and in the intervening years apparently found some way to earn a living. In the summer of 1900, Maurisia bought 160 acres of land in the Mount Diablo meridian off Indian Springs Road. Some eighteen years later, on February 5, 1918, she died at the age of eighty in Santa Barbara. She is buried at the Calvary Cemetery in Santa Barbara, but her tombstone, for reasons unknown, rests at San Carlos Catholic Cemetery in Monterey.

JANE ALLISON

Jane was born in Pennsylvania around 1842, and like so many other madams, she made her entry into the demimonde in San Francisco, but soon moved away, in this case to Santa Cruz. It's not known when, but Jane married William D. Allison, who worked for the California Unfermented Bread Co.[274] By June 1870, she, along with thirty-eight-year-old Emma Cooper and twenty-six-year-old Annie Gonzales, had become saloonkeepers in town. Next door to their saloon was a general merchandise store owned by forty-five-year-old William T. Cooper. In July 1870, Jane's husband was granted a divorce from Jane because of adultery on her part.

In 1872, Jane was arrested in April for keeping a house of ill fame in the city. Officials were so eager to expel Jane from their city that the district attorney subpoenaed 130 witnesses to testify against her.[275] In 1874, it seems Jane went back to San Francisco and was arrested there for using vulgar language, and that's where her story ends.

Epilogue

The stories of these women evoked a rainbow of emotions for me. Some I felt sorry for, some I quickly learned to despise, some gave me nightmares (I bet you know why after reading certain chapters!), and others impressed me.

Living in the wild American West provided women with equal opportunity—for both success and failure. Conventional wisdom suggests that women became prostitutes only because they were desperate. By sharing these stories, I hope you see that this was not always the case. In fact, many of the women were smart entrepreneurs and saw a way to acquire some fast and, in several cases, vast wealth. Despite their reputations in the towns where they lived, these women contributed to the expansion of the great American West.

Endnotes

[1] *San Francisco Chronicle*, March 30, 1889
[2] *Lights and Shades in San Francisco.* San Francisco,
     A.L. Bancroft. 1876
[3] *San Francisco Chronicle*, January 7, 1872
[4] *Daily Alta California*, December 6, 1873
[5] *San Francisco Vindicator*, May 16, 1887
[6] *The San Francisco Call*, September 16, 1892
[7] *Los Angeles Times*, March 7, 1910
[8] U.S. Census Bureau, www.census.gov/population/www/
     documentation/twps0027/tab14.txt, last accessed
     August 10, 2017
[9] *Daily Alta California*, November 26, 1867
[10] *Sacramento Daily Union*, December 2, 1867
[11] *San Francisco Bulletin*, December 3, 1867 and *San Francisco
     Evening Bulletin*, December 24, 1867
[12] *Sacramento Daily Union*, December 4, 1868
[13] *Daily Alta California*, January 22, 1869
[14] Ancestry.com, NY Passenger Lists, February 13, 1869
[15] *Daily Alta California*, September 29, 1870
[16] *Marysville Daily Appeal*, August 18, 1871; *San Francisco
     Evening Bulletin*, August 18, 1871
[17] *San Francisco Chronicle*, July 21, 1871
[18] *Daily Alta California*, February 12, 1880
[19] *San Francisco Evening Bulletin*, April 12, 1883
[20] *San Francisco Chronicle*, January 31, 1883
[21] San Francisco, *The Daily Examiner*, April 12, 1883
[22] San Francisco, *The Daily Examiner*, April 13, 1883
[23] *San Francisco Chronicle*, April 10, 1884
[24] *Daily Alta California*, September 5, 1885

25 *Oakland Daily Evening Tribune*, December 10, 1885

26 *Daily Alta California*, September 11, 1889

27 *Daily Alta, California*, November 21, 1890

28 *Daily Alta California*, November 16, 1871

29 *San Francisco Evening Bulletin*, November 17, 1871

30 *San Francisco Evening Bulletin*, January 28-29, 1872

31 1870 U.S. Census

32 *San Francisco Chronicle*, October 20, 1871

33 *Daily Alta California*, May 16, 1874

34 *San Francisco Chronicle*, July 9, 1875

35 *San Francisco Chronicle*, January 25, 1876

36 San Francisco, *Daily Evening Post*, January 24, 1876

37 *San Francisco Evening Bulletin*, August 1, 1878

38 *San Francisco Evening Bulletin*, August 3, 1878

39 1860 U.S. Census

40 *San Francisco Chronicle*, December 19, 1869

41 *San Francisco Chronicle*, December 19, 1869

42 *San Francisco Chronicle*, December 19, 1869

43 *San Francisco Chronicle*, October 8, 1870

44 *San Francisco Chronicle*, March 9, 1873

45 *Arizona Weekly Journal-Miner*, January 9, 1880

46 *San Francisco Chronicle*, January 22, 1888

47 *The Annals of San Francisco*. Soule, Frank. New York,
     D. Appleton & Co. 1855

48 *Daily Alta California*, March 6, 1851

49 *Daily Alta California*, March 8, 1851

50 Sacramento Transcript, April 9, 1851

51 *Daily Alta California*, May 16 and November 8, 1851

52 *Daily Alta California*, November 9 and 15, 1851

53 *Daily Alta California*, December 11, 1851

54 *Daily Alta California*, December 14 and 15, 1851

55 *Daily Alta California*, February 20, 1852

56 *La Californie: Les Routes Interoceaniques.* Holinksi, Alexander.
     A Labroue Et Compagnie, Imprimeurs, Bruxelles, 1855.
     Translated by Delphine for the author with kindness.

57 *LeCounty & Strong's San Francisco City Directory*, 1854

[58] *Daily Placer Times and Transcript*, March 20, 1855

[59] *San Francisco Evening Bulletin*, November 16, 1855

[60] *Daily Alta California*, October 14, 1871

[61] *Oakland Tribune*, February 2, 1928

[62] *Daily Alta California*, October 3, 1884

[63] *Daily Alta California*, May 8, 1886

[64] *San Francisco Chronicle*, May 3, 1932

[65] *San Francisco Chronicle*, January 12, 1898 and January 29, 1898

[66] *San Francisco Chronicle*, February 24, 1901

[67] *San Francisco Chronicle*, June 15, 1907

[68] *Los Angeles Herald*, December 1, 1908

[69] *The San Francisco Call*, November 7, 1911

[70] *The Madams of San Francisco*. Gentry, Curt. Sausalito, Comstock Editions. 1977

[71] *The Madams of San Francisco*. Gentry, Curt. Sausalito, Comstock Editions. 1977

[72] *San Francisco Chronicle*, May 25, 1918

[73] *Sacramento Bee*, April 29, 1932

[74] *The Madams of San Francisco*. Gentry, Curt. Sausalito, Comstock Editions. 1977

[75] *San Francisco Chronicle*, June 8, 1917

[76] *San Francisco Chronicle*, December 19, 1917

[77] *The Madams of San Francisco*. Gentry, Curt. Sausalito, Comstock Editions. 1977

[78] *Oakland Tribune*, April 10, 1910

[79] *The Madams of San Francisco*. Gentry, Curt. Sausalito, Comstock Editions. 1977

[80] *San Francisco Chronicle*, May 29, 1917

[81] *Oakland Tribune*, August 5, 1912

[82] *Oakland Tribune*, February 22, 1917

[83] *San Francisco Chronicle*, May 15, 1917

[84] *San Francisco Chronicle*, May 29, 1917

[85] *The Madams of San Francisco*. Gentry, Curt. Sausalito, Comstock Editions. 1977

[86] *San Francisco Chronicle*, May 18, 1917

[87] *San Francisco Chronicle*, December 19, 1917

[88] *San Francisco Chronicle,* April 29, 1932

[89] Fold3.com, last accessed August 17, 2017

[90] Ancestry.com, last accessed August 16, 2017

[91] www.findagrave.com and www.ancestry.com, last accessed
    August 29, 2017

[92] Author conversation with Greenlawn Cemetery staff
    August 16, 2017

[93] *San Francisco Chronicle,* May 7, 1905

[94] *San Francisco Chronicle,* August 6, 1902

[95] *The San Francisco Call,* June 3, 1903

[96] *Oakland Tribune,* May 27, 1905 and *The Tacoma Times,*
    July 4, 1904

[97] *The San Francisco Call,* May 9, 1905

[98] *Oakland Tribune,* May 13, 1905

[99] *Oakland Tribune,* May 27, 1905

[100] *The San Francisco Call,* November 8, 1906

[101] *The San Francisco Call,* September 6, 1906 and January 26, 1907

[102] *The San Francisco Call,* February 14, 1907

[103] *San Francisco Chronicle,* May 7, 1907

[104] *The San Francisco Call,* August 21, 1908

[105] *San Francisco Chronicle,* February 15, 1908

[106] *The San Francisco Call,* August 26, 1908

[107] *Call House Madam.* Wolsey, Serge. San Francisco,
    Martin Trousdale Corp. 1945

[108] Ancestry.com, last accessed September 1, 2017. Ship manifest.

[109] *San Francisco Chronicle,* October 29, 1923

[110] *Santa Cruz News,* April 2, 1923

[111] *Evening Bulletin* (San Francisco, CA), August 18, 1877

[112] *Sacramento Daily Union,* August 11, 1870

[113] *Sacramento Daily Union,* April 2, 1872

[114] *Sacramento Daily Union,* August 18, 1873

[115] *Sacramento Daily Union,* January 1, 1875

[116] *Sacramento Daily Union,* September 5, 1866

[117] *The Daily Bee,* November 2, 1869

[118] Ancestry.com, accessed September 14, 2017

119 *The Sacramento Directory, H.S. Crocker*, 1871, Ancestry.com,
    last accessed September 4, 2018

120 *Sacramento Daily Union*, August 18, 1873

121 Ancestry.com, last accessed September 14, 2017

122 *Record-Union*, June 18, 1898

123 *Sacramento Daily Union*, October 17, 1868

124 *San Francisco Chronicle*, October 11, 1868

125 *Sacramento Daily Union*, February 25, 1870

126 *Sacramento Daily Union*, August 18, 1870

127 *Sacramento Daily Union*, November 23, 1875

128 Ancestry.com, accessed September 12, 2017

129 *Sacramento Daily Union*, May 12, 1873

130 *Sacramento Daily Union*, May 9, 1873

131 *Red Bluff Independent*, October 25, 1873

132 *San Francisco Chronicle*, October 27, 1873

133 *Red Bluff Independent*, October 25, 1873

134 *Los Angeles Herald*, April 24, 1886

135 Los Angeles Almanac, www.laalmanac.com/population/po02.php,
    last accessed July 27, 2017

136 *The Daily Examiner*, August 28, 1887

137 *The Daily Examiner*, August 28, 1887

138 *San Francisco Chronicle*, September 10, 1887

139 *Los Angeles Herald*, March 31, 1896

140 *Los Angeles Herald*, August 12, 1897

141 *Los Angeles Herald*, September 29, 1897

142 *Call House Madam*. Wolsey, Serge. San Francisco,
    Martin Tudordale Corp. 1945

143 *Call House Madam*. Wolsey, Serge. San Francisco,
    Martin Tudordale Corp. 1945

144 *Hollywood Madam*. Francis, Lee. Los Angeles, Holloway House. ..
    1987

145 *Call House Madam*. Wolsey, Serge. San Francisco,
    Martin Trousdale Corp. 1945

146 *The San Francisco Call*, March 14, 1911

147 *Hollywood Madam*. Francis, Lee. Los Angeles, Holloway House. ..
    1987

148 *Call House Madam*. Wolsey, Serge. San Francisco,
      Martin Trousdale Corp. 1945
149 *Hollywood Madam*. Francis, Lee. Los Angeles, Holloway House.
      1987
150 *Los Angeles Times*, June 19, 1945
151 *Los Angeles Times*, May 11, 1946
152 *Los Angeles Times*, December 17, 1947
153 *Call House Madam*. Wolsey, Serge. San Francisco,
      Martin Trousdale Corp. 1945
154 *Pasadena Independent*, August 16, 1960
155 *Santa Cruz Sentinel*, December 17, 1870
156 *Fresno Weekly Republican*, October 26, 1888
157 *Daily Morning Republican*, June 23, 1889
158 *Fresno Weekly Republican*, March 22, 1889
159 *Daily Morning Republican*, June 16, 1889
160 *Daily Morning Republican*, June 19, 1889
161 *Daily Morning Republican*, June 21, 1889
162 *Fresno Weekly Republican*, July 12, 1889
163 *Fresno Weekly Republican*, July 12, 1889
164 *San Francisco Chronicle*, July 12, 1889
165 *Sacramento Daily Record-Union*, August 3, 1889
166 *Fresno Weekly Republican*, July 23, 1889
167 *San Francisco Chronicle*, July 26, 1889
168 *Los Angeles Herald*, August 4, 1889
169 *Fresno Weekly Republican*n, July 26, 1889
170 *Daily Morning Republican*, October 13, 1889
171 *Fresno Weekly Republican*, January 17, 1890
172 *Fresno Weekly Republican*, January 17, 1890
173 *Fresno Weekly Republican*, January 17, 1890
174 *Fresno Weekly Republican*, February 14, 1890
175 *Daily Morning Republican*, February 12, 1890
176 *Daily Morning Republican*, February 6, 1890
177 *Fresno Weekly Republican*, March 14, 1890
178 *Daily Morning Republican*, March 9, 1890
179 *Daily Morning Republican*, January 1, 1891
180 *Daily Morning Republican*, July 23, 1898

181 *Healdsburg Enterprise*, February 12, 1916

182 *Daily Evening Post*, May 19, 1875

183 *Sacramento Daily Union*, April 17, 1861

184 *New York Tribune*, November 1861

185 *Marysville Daily Appeal*, December 14, 1861

186 *New London Daily Chronicle*, New London, CT,
     November 4, 1861

187 *The Patriot*, Harrisburg, PA, November 7, 1861

188 *The Press*, Philadelphia, PA, November 12, 1861

189 *San Francisco Bulletin*, February 10, 1864

190 *San Francisco Bulletin*, October 10, 1864

191 *Marysville Daily Appeal*, September 13, 1862

192 *Daily Alta California*, May 17, 1855

193 *Daily Alta California*, July 27, 1885

194 *Daily Alta California*, May 17, 1855

195 *Daily Alta California*, May 17, 1855

196 *Daily Alta California*, July 27, 1885

197 *Daily Alta California*, November 3, 1855

198 *San Francisco Evening Bulletin*, August 23, 1856

199 *Sacramento Daily Union*, October 12, 1859

200 *Sacramento Daily Union*, February 5, 1867

201 *San Francisco Chronicle*, May 9, 1871

202 *Daily Alta California*, May 16, 1874

203 *Placer Argus*, July 23 and 30, 1885, www.genealogytrails.com/
     cal/placer/obit/KMobits_C.html, last accessed August 3, 2017

204 *The Sun*, San Diego, December 21, 1881

205 *The Sun*, San Diego, November 30, 1881

206 *The San Diego Union*, October 14, 1887

207 *Coronado Evening Mercury*, October 14, 1887

208 *San Diego Daily Sun*, February 7, 1888,

209 *San Diego Sun*, February 7, 1888

210 *San Diego Union*, March 9, 1887

211 *San Diego Daily Bee*, December 6, 1887

212 *Sacramento Daily Union*, June 29, 1887

213 *San Diego Union*, June 28, 1887

214 *Coronado Mercury*, June 29, 1887

215 *Coronado Mercury*, July 9, 1887

216 *San Francisco Chronicle*, September 2, 1887

217 *San Diego Union*, May 13, 1887

218 *San Francisco Chronicle*, August 8, 1888

219 *San Francisco Chronicle*, August 17, 1887

220 *San Francisco Chronicle*, August 10, 1888

221 *San Diego Union*, August 11, 1887

222 *Coronado Mercury*, September 1, 1887

223 *San Francisco Chronicle*, December 14, 1887

224 *San Francisco Chronicle*, April 26, 1888

225 *San Francisco Bulletin*, July 6, 1888

226 *San Diego Union*, July 7, 1887

227 *San Francisco Chronicle*, August 11, 1888

228 *San Diego Union*, March 11, 1887

229 *San Diego Daily Sun*, February 22, 1888

230 *Monteith's Directory of San Diego*, 1889

231 *San Diego Union*, September 13, 15, and 22, 1891

232 *Directory of San Diego*, 1892, Archive.org, last accessed August 29, 2018

233 *San Diego Union*, March 10, 1899

234 *Evening Tribune*, April 14, 1899

235 1899 business directory, Ancestry.com, last accessed August 23, 2018

236 *San Diego Union*, June 18, 1899

237 *San Diego Union*, October 2, 1901

238 *San Diego Union*, March 18, 1902

239 *San Diego Union*, April 12, 1902

240 *San Diego Union*, April 24, 1902

241 Jerry MacMullen interview, *The Journal of San Diego History*, Fall 1981, sandiegohistory.org, last accessed August 28, 2018

242 Jerry MacMullen interview, *The Journal of San Diego History*, Fall 1981, sandiegohistory.org, last accessed August 28, 2018

243 *Evening Tribune*, June 11, 1904

244 *Evening Tribune*, August 4, 1904

245 *Evening Tribune*, September 20 and 26, 1904

246 Copy of marriage entry from St. Joseph's, San Diego, CA

247 *San Diego Union*, January 16, 1907

248 *San Diego Union*, January 17, 1907

249 *San Diego Union*, May 4, 1907

250 Mount Hope Cemetery records, confirmed August 30, 2018

251 *San Diego City and County Directory*, 1907 and 1908, Archives.... org, last accessed August 28, 2018

252 *Evening Tribune*, October 29, 1910

253 *San Diego Union*, April 28, 1921

254 *Evening Tribune*, September 21, 1922

255 Jerry MacMullen interview, *The Journal of San Diego History*, Fall 1981, sandiegohistory.org, last accessed August 28, 2018

256 *Evening Tribune*, February 22, 1923

257 *San Diego Union*, April 8, 1923

258 *Riverside Daily Press*, January 7, 1924

259 U.S. City Directories, 1918, Ancestry.com

260 San Jose *Evening News*, March 17, 1885

261 San Jose *Evening News*, December 14, 1886

262 San Jose *Evening News*, September 28, 1887

263 *San Francisco Chronicle*, September 22, 1883

264 San Jose *Evening News*, May 20, 1886

265 San Jose *Evening News*, May 4, 1895

266 San Jose *Evening News*, May 17, 1895

267 San Jose *Evening News*, May 27, 1895

268 San Jose *Evening News*, August 26, 1898

269 San Jose *Evening News*, February 11, 1888

270 *Santa Cruz Sentinel*, November 18, 1871

271 *San Luis Obispo Tribune*, January 17, 1884

272 *San Luis Obispo Tribune*, December 17, 1881

273 *San Luis Obispo Tribune*, February 2 and December 4, 1883

274 *San Francisco Directory*, 1868. Ancestry.com, last accessed September 14, 2017

275 *San Francisco Chronicle*, April 27, 1872

Index

Macs. *See* pimps
Madam Mack. *See* Marks, Hanchen
madams, v–viii; attitudes toward, 53–54, 64, 77; charitable character of, 100, 101, 103–104, 117, 123; corruption and, 14; desperation of, 134; elusiveness of, 27, 116, 126; ethnicity of, 92, 94; hiring practices of, 15, 47; law and, 13, 46, 48, 54, 77, 127; marriages and divorces of, 67; in mining camps, 91, 94; as renters, 80; romantic interests of, 58. *See also names of individual madams*
Madera, CA, 88
Major Hufeland (pigeon), 121–122
Malty (cat), 121–122
Manchuria (ship), 49
Mansfield, Saddie, 19
maquereaux. See pimps
Marcus, Ivoal (Ivoal Marve), 121
Marcus, Josephine Sarah (Josephine Sarah Earp), 16
The Marion, 121
Market Street (San Francisco), 5, 10, 18, 27, **28**, 38
Markham, William Hogg Wolseley, 65–66
Marks, Aaron, 94–95
Marks, Dora, 98
Marks, Hanchen, 94–98
Martin, Virginia (Virginia Morton), 121
Martin Tudordale, Inc., 75
Marve, Ivoal (Ivoal Marcus), 121
Mary Antoinette (prostitute), 55
Marysville, CA, 91–92
May, Lulu, 15–16
May, Tallie, 15–16
McCann, Teddy Ann. *See* McCarron, Teddy
McCarron, Teddy, 110–111
McCarthy, Dave, 18
McCarthy, Dennis, 112, 113–114
McCarthy, Jeremiah, 40
McCarthy, Joseph Lawrence (Joseph Lawrence Wall), 26–27, 40–41
McCarthy, Maria, 27, 40–41

McConnell, Lizzie, 10
McElroy, Clara, 103
McKay, Albert, 27
McLendon, Annie. *See* Bailey, Ida
McLendon, William Boyd, 119–121
Mellon, Anna May. *See* Hayman, Jessie
Mellon, Jessie. *See* Hayman, Jessie
Merchant's Carnival, 80
Merrifield, Frank, 13
Meyer, Freida, 117
Midget (prostitute), 86
Miller, M. M., 26
Miller, W. B., 55
miners, vi, 53, 91, **92**, 131
mining communities, 91–94
Mission District (San Francisco), 26
Monahan, Officer, 128
Monterey, CA, 131, 133, 134
Mooney, John, 28–30, **29**
moral crusade, 46–47, 54, 68, 77–79, 108–109, 111, 117, 119, 126–127
Morgan, Constable, 87
Morton, Josephine, 35
Morton, Virginia (Virginia Martin), 121
Mother Superior (Los Angeles), 69
motion picture industry, 64
Murasky, Judge, 30
murders, 32, 59–60, 73, 94, 97–98, 117, 123
Murphy, Dr., 6
Murphy, Judge, 11
Murphy, Mary, 91
Murphy, William, 32
Myrick, Milton, 15–16

N
Nazareth House, 123
Nellie (prostitute), 6
Nelson, Robert, 23
Nelson Lodgings, 27
Neumann, P. (prostitute), 43
Nevine, Maggie M., 48
"The New Evangel," 61
Newell, Ed, 34
Nora (friend of Lee Francis), 71–72

About the Author

S herry's passion for food, travel, people, and history led her to create her first book, *Taste of Tombstone*, in 1998. That same passion landed her a monthly food column in *True West* magazine starting in 2009. Since then she's penned several books on the Victorian West and multiple magazine features.

She is a past president of Western Writers of America and holds memberships in the James Beard Foundation, the Author's Guild, Single Action Shooting Society, and the Wild West History Association. Sherry is one of the original members of the Most Intrepid Western Author Posse and was sworn in as honorary Dodge City marshal during one of the "rides."

Sherry has earned Will Rogers Gold Medallions for her *Cowboy's Cookbook* and *Tinsel, Tumbleweeds, and Star-Spangled Celebrations*, and a bronze for *Golden Elixir of the West*. She also earned a Wrangler for her appearance in a Wyatt Earp documentary.